Rape Culture in the House of David

Rape Culture in the House of David: A Company of Men describes a biblical rape culture sustained and maintained by Yhwh and a host of men—from royal kings and princes to their relatives, counselors, generals, and servants.

This volume reveals that sexual violence in the house of David is not simply perpetrated by its most powerful men. Rather, in the pursuit of power, status, authority, and honor, men form alliances and networks that support the use and abuse of women's bodies and valorize sexualized violence against other men. The man who is most capable of sexual violence is Israel's ideal king.

Barbara Thiede deftly addresses the power and contemporary relevance of these narratives and argues that exposing and naming rape culture in biblical literature is essential—in social, economic, and political realms.

This is a meaningful feminist intervention in the field of biblical studies and is of great benefit to graduate students and scholars of religion, gender studies, and masculinity studies.

Barbara Thiede is Professor of Religious Studies at the University of North Carolina at Charlotte, USA.

Rape Culture, Religion and the Bible
Series Editors:
Caroline Blyth
University of Auckland, New Zealand
Johanna Stiebert
University of Leeds, UK

Rape Myths, the Bible and #MeToo
Johanna Stiebert

Telling Terror in Judges 19
Rape and Reparation for the Levite's wife
Helen Paynter

Resisting Rape Culture
The Hebrew Bible and Hong Kong Sex Workers
Nany Nan Hoon Tan

The Bible and Sexual Violence Against Men
Chris Greenough

Rape Culture, Purity Culture, and Coercive Control in Teen Girl Bibles
Caroline Blyth

Trafficking Hadassah
Collective Trauma, Cultural Memory, and Identity in the Book of Esther and in the African Diaspora
Ericka Shawndricka Dunbar

Vocation and Violence
The Church and #MeToo
Miryam Clough

For more information about this series, please visit: www.routledge.com/Rape-Culture-Religion-and-the-Bible/book-series/RCRB

Rape Culture in the House of David

A Company of Men

Barbara Thiede

LONDON AND NEW YORK

First published 2022
by Routledge
4 Park Square, Milton Park, Abingdon, Oxon OX14 4RN

and by Routledge
605 Third Avenue, New York, NY 10158

Routledge is an imprint of the Taylor & Francis Group, an informa business

© 2022 Barbara Thiede

The right of Barbara Thiede to be identified as author of this work has been asserted in accordance with sections 77 and 78 of the Copyright, Designs and Patents Act 1988.

All rights reserved. No part of this book may be reprinted or reproduced or utilised in any form or by any electronic, mechanical, or other means, now known or hereafter invented, including photocopying and recording, or in any information storage or retrieval system, without permission in writing from the publishers.

Trademark notice: Product or corporate names may be trademarks or registered trademarks, and are used only for identification and explanation without intent to infringe.

British Library Cataloguing-in-Publication Data
A catalogue record for this book is available from the British Library

Library of Congress Cataloging-in-Publication Data
Names: Thiede, Barbara, author.
Title: Rape culture in the House of David : a company of men / Barbara Thiede.
Description: Abingdon, Oxon ; New York, NY : Routledge, 2022. | Series: Rape culture, religion and the Bible | Includes bibliographical references and index.
Identifiers: LCCN 2022002638 (print) | LCCN 2022002639 (ebook) | ISBN 9780367857615 (hbk) | ISBN 9781032302218 (pbk) | ISBN 9781003014911 (ebk)
Subjects: LCSH: Bible. Samuel—Criticism, interpretation, etc. | Rape in the Bible. | Sex in the Bible.
Classification: LCC BS1325.6.R27 T45 2022 (print) | LCC BS1325.6.R27 (ebook) | DDC 220.8/3641532—dc23/eng/20220304
LC record available at https://lccn.loc.gov/2022002638
LC ebook record available at https://lccn.loc.gov/2022002639

ISBN: 978-0-367-85761-5 (hbk)
ISBN: 978-1-032-30221-8 (pbk)
ISBN: 978-1-003-01491-1 (ebk)

DOI: 10.4324/9781003014911

Typeset in Times New Roman
by Apex CoVantage, LLC

For Erik Henning and Ralf
לחכם לב יקרא נבון
Proverbs 16:21

Contents

Acknowledgements   viii

Introduction: Rape and Rape Culture in the Hebrew Bible: Choosing the Right Words   1

1 Disposing of Daughters, Sisters, and Wives: The Rapes of Tamar and of David's *Pilagshim*   22

2 The Taking, Trapping, and Raping of Women: Michal and Bathsheba   46

3 The Once and the Future King: Saul, David, and the Practice of Sexual Violence   74

Hidden in Plain Sight—The Rape Culture of the Hebrew Bible: Conclusions   100

Author and Subject Index   105
Index of Biblical References   109

Acknowledgements

Thanks are due to Joanne Maguire, my Department Chair, for her unswerving support. It sustains me. My students deserve the same gratitude for their curiosity and courage; they never fail to make me reconsider what I imagine I know.

The best editor enters the mind and understands the intention of an author. Such editors strengthen, sharpen, and extend the work. I had two such editors and my luck and gratitude cannot be overstated. My thanks to Johanna Stiebert and Caroline Blyth. Their support, sophistication, and consummate knowledge did much to shape this work.

Erik Henning Thiede repeatedly prompted me to fast forward my thinking; Ralf Thiede posed subtle questions that shifted and renewed my understanding. These two men know what drives me. And so, I am made whole in this work.

Introduction

Rape and Rape Culture in the Hebrew Bible: Choosing the Right Words

Introduction

Acts of sexual violence are not outliers. Sexual violence is omnipresent in social media, literature, art, and music worldwide. It is a global practice. Date rape, gang rape, spousal rape, child rape, serial rape, revenge rape, war rape, genocidal rape, exchange rape, ceremonial rape . . . the list is a long one. It is even possible to commit sexual assault through words and images. Deepfake porn, which deploys machine learning and artificial intelligence to place victims' faces on actors' bodies, is now an industry. Women, who are the most common victims of technology-based sexual violence,[1] go into hiding, lose their jobs, or commit suicide. They are raped by proxy, and, sometimes, assaulted physically.[2]

Rape culture transcends gender and age. Men denude and humiliate each other sexually; American service men did so to their prisoners in Abu Ghraib.[3] Almost half of transgender people have been sexually assaulted, and the number rises for trans people of color and those who have a disability, are homeless, or who have worked in the sex industry.[4] Sexual assault against children and the elderly is likewise a ubiquitous presence in our time.[5]

Contemporary rape cultures are underwritten by texts considered sacred and holy across the globe—and those include the Hebrew Bible.[6] Even in secular realms, these texts have had an outsized influence on cultural products, from literature and film to television and internet sites. The secular, cultural, and religious authorities who ignore, downplay, or dare to romanticize the sexual violence in the pages of the Hebrew Bible do so with material consequence. To rationalize, justify, and even glorify sexual violence in texts that *support* religious communities and *influence* secular cultures is to rationalize, justify, and even glorify sexual violence that *occurs* in religious communities and secular cultures. Academics and religious leaders alike must consider the consequences.

DOI: 10.4324/9781003014911-1

For this reason, then, *Rape Culture in the House of David: A Company of Men* describes, explores, and interrogates the rape culture we find in the pages of the Books of Samuel. In these texts, family members, royal counselors, friends, retainers, and servants exploit the "right" to rape. Men help plan rape, they enable rape, and they watch rape. The men around David and his sons participate vicariously in sexual violence against women, and they shield the royal rapists they serve. Male characters commit sexualized violence against men, too, symbolically raping their enemies by defeating them in battle and then mutilating their bodies.

The Hebrew Bible is, like the rape cultures of our time, filled with images and acts of sexual violence. Female characters are handed over to foreign potentates for their use (Gen. 12) or made the objects of the male gaze in exhibitionist displays arranged by their husbands (Gen. 26). Virgin girls who have not "known a man" are offered to mobs intent on gang rape (Gen. 19:8; Judg. 19:24; 21:20–23). A young woman, perhaps barely out of girlhood, is handed over by her husband to men who torture and rape her all night (Judg. 19:25). A woman's raped body may be discarded at will—in this particular case, the woman is butchered, her body pieces sent throughout the land by the husband who threw her to a gang of rapists in the first place (19:29).

The Israelite deity Yhwh, too, is a perpetrator of sexual violence. In the Book of Lamentations, he orchestrates the gang rape of Daughter Zion by the nations (1:9–10). His personified and female spouse, Israel, suffers brutal and sexualized punishment at his hands when he strips Israel and exposes her, placing her before a violent mob to be stoned and stabbed (Ezek. 16:27–41). Similarly, Yhwh condemns his former lovers Oholah (Samaria) and Oholibah (Jerusalem) to mutilation and stoning (Ezek. 23).[7]

Female characters are not the only victims of sexual violence in the Hebrew Bible. Some men are threatened with rape, such as Lot in Genesis 19 and the Levite in Judges 19.[8] Suzanne Scholz argues that Yhwh rapes Job in 30:11 (2017, 177), and Emma Nagouse suggests that the *gever*, the strong man of Lamentations 3, experiences a divine rape (2018, 146). Men can be symbolically raped while being murdered; Ehud drives his dagger so deeply into King Eglon's belly that his enemy's flesh swallows even the hilt (Judg. 3:21–22).[9] Yael will likewise drive a phallic tent peg into Sisera's head (Judg. 4–5).[10] Kings and generals show how good they are at being a man by feminizing and symbolically raping other men. They humiliate their enemies, cut off their body parts, slice off their foreskins (Judg. 1:6–7; 1 Sam. 18:27), and decapitate them (1 Sam. 17:50–51; 2 Sam. 4:7–8). In biblical culture, men defeated in battle are considered men who have been raped (Niditch 2008, 6).[11] Men who are mutilated after death in battle are, in effect, raped twice. Rape—in at least metaphorical terms—is not so exceptional for male characters of the Hebrew Bible as we might assume. The rape of men in physical terms is not unknown to its authors either.

Given the pervasive depiction of sexual violence in the Hebrew Bible as a whole, it should hardly surprise readers that David and his sons exercise power and authority using the self-same tactics. As we will see, women are assaulted in word and deed. King Saul calls his wife a cunt in front of a host of men (1 Sam. 20:30). King David is joined by a servant or courtier in ogling Bathsheba as she washes herself, and then, like powerful men of our time do, he sends other men to bring her to him for his sexual use (2 Sam. 11:2–4). King Solomon far outdoes his father in acquiring women, ceasing only when he has procured 1,000 wives and *pilagshim* for his sexual use (1 Kings 11:3).[12]

We encounter ugly scenes of sexual assault in the Books of Samuel. David's first son, Amnon, puts his half-sister, Tamar, on sexual display for other men. He sends away servants, friends, and courtiers before the rape but they remain within hearing range, on call to help dispose of his victim when he is finished with her. David's third son, Absalom, rapes his father's women out in the open, on the same roof where David himself had previously played Peeping Tom. Absalom ensures that other men can watch as he violates David's *pilagshim*. The Books of Samuel depict rape with regularity.

Rape Culture: A (Justified) Term for the Hebrew Bible?

Rape culture is defined by the ubiquitous presence of sexual assault and sexual violence—most typically, though not exclusively, against women.[13] Its depiction is pervasive, and its practice is embedded in contemporary discourses. This is precisely what we also find in the biblical world. Biblical authors portray male characters who use language to strip and humiliate women in front of other men. Kings, princes, soldiers, and tribesmen send for, seize, and assault women. The men of the Hebrew Bible prove their power, their status, and their rank by committing sexualized violence against other men too. Sexual violence is not simply a byproduct of biblical systems of power—it is a necessary component of those systems. Men become men through using women's bodies and through humiliating men who challenge their authority. Violence is, as Harold Washington notes, "central to the consolidation of masculine identity" (1998, 186). Sharing, raping, destroying, and even butchering women to achieve power and rank is not simply par for the course, it makes the course possible in the first place.[14]

Nevertheless, many scholars suggest that applying the words "rape" and "rape culture" to texts of the Hebrew Bible is problematic at best and a gross mistake at worst. The academy, after all, values analyzing texts in their own contexts, according to the presumed premises of their time. We moderns are retrojecting, committing thought crimes, if we use current terminology and concepts to discuss texts written thousands of years before we were born. "Applying modern categories or definitions of rape . . . serves little purpose," writes Leah Rediger Schulte (2017, 143).[15] We need to understand the world biblical authors describe on *their* terms. Such authors, scholars may argue, do not entertain the idea of consent, they have no specific word for rape, and they do not understand taking a woman as a violent act but rather as a male right that is only limited by the rights of other men. They do not think like we do.

Indeed, biblical authors did not imagine that their female characters had the agency to grant or refuse men access to their bodies. In biblical texts, after all, only adult men possess full legal status. Male transactions, whether political, economic, social, or sexual, are what matter; legal codes, narratives, poetry, and proverbs make male rights their concern. Sexual access to women is legislated; it comes with terms and conditions. A man may not have sexual access to another man's wife (Deut. 22:22). He may not have sexual contact with a woman who is betrothed (22:23–25). He may not use a virgin sexually, though if he does, he must pay an indemnity to her father before she becomes his wife (22:28–29).[16]

Scholars rightfully claim that female consent is, for biblical authors, effectively a non-issue.[17] Robert S. Kawashima states:

> If the modern concept of forcible rape is defined as a nonconsensual sexual encounter in which the "object" of the encounter is also its "victim"—the one whose rights have been violated—then there was no such thing as forcible rape in biblical Israel's legal system.
>
> (2011, 2)

It is merely "illicit sex." The crime's victim is not the woman, but either her father or her husband (ibid).[18] Kawashima concludes that the body of biblical literature makes it clear that women have no right to refuse any sexual advance (3). It appears to follow, then, that scholars cannot apply a modern understanding of rape to biblical texts.

Other scholars define a notion of rape in the Bible, but one they limit to what they believe the texts themselves admit. "Biblical scholars must have a definition of biblical rape *qua* biblical rape in order to engage its meaning in an ancient context," writes Schulte (2017, 10). Alexander Izuchukwu Abasili agrees, arguing that while biblical authors do have an idea of rape, "Hebrew-biblical rape" is clearly defined as the "'physical' use of power by a man in overpowering a woman into non-consensual sexual intercourse."

"The force in question here," Abasili writes, "may or may not be psychological or social or political or emotional, but must be physical/violent" (2011, 6). According to this perspective, Bathsheba is not explicitly and clearly the victim of a violent attack by David and thus we cannot call what happened to her a rape (*passim*). David's daughter Tamar, in contrast, is described as the victim of physical and violent acts on the part of her half-brother Amnon and can therefore be considered a victim of rape (4).

Schulte provides a definition for "biblical rape" based on four required elements. She concludes that we can identify a rape in the Bible only when the following features are clearly present in the text: the rapists must be foreigners or outsiders; the deity must be wholly absent from the scene; rape is necessarily related to evidence that Israelites are ignoring their covenantal responsibilities with Yhwh; and the whole event is bound to the application of incorrect solutions. Thus, for Schulte, too, Bathsheba could not have been raped. Why? Because the deity only appears at the end of her story (2017, 144).

Similarly, in her monograph *Sexual Transgression in the Hebrew Bible*, Hilary B. Lipka claims that readers can determine a biblical author is articulating a concept of rape when two conditions are clearly fulfilled in the text at hand: the author must depict a sexual act that has, first, been forced on an unwilling victim and, secondly, results in emotional trauma (2006, 202). Lipka frequently finds that neither of these two conditions apply. She thus concludes that the range of legal and narrative texts she studies should largely be understood as "sexual transgression" rather than "rape."

A host of scholars, then, have argued that the Hebrew Bible presents ideas wholly different from our own about what constitutes sexual assault, or rape. They suggest that, for biblical writers, a man who accesses a woman's body on the wrong terms is not in most cases guilty of rape, but of "illicit" or "transgressive" sex. Modern observers, therefore, should only call scenes of sexual violence "rape" in a few, very narrowly defined circumstances. According to this view, contemporary readers must therefore confine themselves to describing sexual violence in the biblical texts using the language of the authors. In other words, we can call it only what the writers call it and name it only according to their premises.

Certainly scholars need to understand as best they can the language of ancient texts, the agendas of their authors, and what is so often called the "historical context." And yet, any attempt to explain sexual assault and sexual violence in biblical authors' terms leads to a host of disturbing consequences. First, those interpreters who strive to be "objective" and "scientific" still impose their own premises on the material. We all do. Second, when texts of the Hebrew Bible are contorted to fit a mold the scholar constructs for "biblical rape," the result is tautological. Third, scholars who are concerned about the application of the terms "rape" and "rape culture" frequently collude with the texts, suggesting that they don't understand how either of these terms works.

Lipka's arguments, for example, demonstrate what happens when scholars, while claiming objectivity, nevertheless retroject their own contemporary assumptions. To use the term "rape," she argues, we must know that the author himself considered the sex he describes as an act of force committed against the will of the victim and that the act clearly resulted in emotional trauma for the victim (2006, 220). As Susanne Scholz cautions, Lipka is relying on a modern assumption that it is "possible, desirable, and relatively obvious to know what the original authors thought about sexual violence. The second requirement prioritizes the individualism of the victim-survivor, yet another modern assumption" (2019, 24).

It is, moreover, hard to know what to do with those requirements. Of course, biblical authors were capable of describing victims of sexual assault as deeply distressed and traumatized. They do so, for example, in the case of Tamar's rape in 2 Samuel 13 and Oholibah's rape in Ezekiel 23:22–44. But how would a scholar prove that the 400 women taken from their slaughtered families in Judges 21 were emotionally distressed by their experience? The author has nothing to say about their reactions because they do not matter. His agenda is to describe how the Benjaminites can acquire the female bodies they need for the tribe to survive. For that author, Israel must become whole again to serve Yhwh. How the men of the tribes achieve that end is the focus of the narrative; how the captured women feel is irrelevant. It is worse than tone-deaf to insist that the biblical author must describe the emotional trauma of these victims so we can name what happens to them sexual assault.

In Schulte's case, the search for some "biblical definition" of rape leads to establishing conditions that seem at best awkward and at worst dangerous. If we follow her specifications to their logical conclusion, the Israelite soldier who takes a woman as a prisoner and uses her body sexually until he no longer has any use for her (Deut. 21:10–14) cannot possibly be regarded as a rapist. He is not a "foreigner," after all. Effectively, Schulte's conditions throw out any interrogation of this text. Given condemnations of modern soldiers who capture, abuse, and discard female captives, creating an exclusion clause for an ancient Israelite doing the very same is a slippery move indeed.

In positing a definition of "biblical rape," Abasili argues that the biblical author must employ language that clearly refers to the use of physical force. David may ogle Bathsheba and have her brought to his palace for sexual use, but this cannot count as rape. In this narrative, however, a woman is brought to a powerful man *at his command and in order for him to use her body sexually*. Would modern-day scholars, upon hearing or reading about women, children, and men in our world who have been moved from one location to another so that a powerful man could use their bodies sexually, regard such actions as harmless erotic play? Such control of others' bodies, through the use of power and authority, is *exactly* how men commit sexual assault. The very things that make rape possible—male power to move others' bodies at will and to use them sexually at will, and the victims' inability to have any control over what happens—are features of a text Abasili wants to declare rape free.

Just try imagining (and this will be easy) that you live in a culture in which all manner of sexual violence exists. This violence is depicted in every artistic and social medium available. It finds expression in the ways men speak about women and their bodies in a wide range of settings, from their offices to their Facebook and Twitter accounts. It is used to dehumanize people of color and LGBTQ+ individuals. It is a tool for preying on children, the elderly, the poor and disempowered who work in the most menial and vulnerable of professions. In this world, those who control others with misogynistic behaviors, with sexual violence, and with rape and gang rape generally pay no price. And now, after you have imagined this culture (which is your own), ask yourself whether the purveyors of this culture—the (mostly) cisgender heterosexual men who collude in making sexual violence everywhere acceptable and permissible—are likely to tell you, "Yes, absolutely. I live in a *rape culture*—no question about it!"

In the United States, where I was born and raised, Donald Trump bragged about grabbing women "by the pussy" and later excused his language as "locker room banter." Harvey Weinstein, convicted of raping a number of women, was accused by assistants, models, script writers and readers, and aspiring and established Hollywood actresses who described a pattern of sexual assault that spanned three decades. Despite his use of non-disclosure agreements to silence his victims, he claimed that every woman who accused him of sexual assault had gladly consented to have sex with him. Sexual harassers are most likely to insist they had no idea they were doing anything wrong. The day such perpetrators solemnly tell any of us that they live in a rape culture might be the day on which we could start dismantling what they have wrought.

How does it escape scholars' notice that denying a woman any power over any kind of consent is a *defining feature* of rape culture?[19] Why is it difficult to understand that the very lack of a specific term for "rape" in the Hebrew Bible, coupled with the abundance of sexual violence in its texts, is *evidence* of a rape culture par excellence, not of its absence? Sexual violence is legislated (Deut. 22), encouraged (Judg. 21), and facilitated because biblical systems depend upon its existence to function. Kawashima's claim that biblical law and literature "failed to perceive" what he calls "forcible" rape is absurd. In fact, just the opposite is true: biblical law and literature *sanction* rape. In that world, rape is useful. It permits men to control men through the threat of physical rape and through acts of symbolic rape. It permits male characters to share, assault, and discard women's bodies in order to generate male-male alliances, friendships, and partnerships. Rape is a strategy for establishing rank, power, and status among men. Without rape, the Hebrew Bible as we know it, would be a fundamentally different set of texts.[20]

Erasure, Silencing, and Collusion: How *Not* to Read the Hebrew Bible

The term "rape culture" is, by its very nature, a judgment call. It is a term of resistance. It is not a term that those who create, sustain, and perpetuate rape cultures would use about their environments or about the systems within which they operate. If we can point to explicit descriptions of men dehumanizing others through sexually violent language, if we can see sexualized violence and sexual assault permeating the pages of any text we read, and if we can recognize that the discourse within those pages valorizes sexual violence, then we would be colluding in every part of that if we *didn't* name what we see as what it is: a rape culture.

Colluding with the rape culture of the Hebrew Bible achieves erasure. It silences. Calling sexual violence of the Hebrew Bible "illicit sex" or "sexual transgression" repeats and recycles the Hebrew Bible's tolerance, acceptance, and, ultimately, valorization of rape. Calling an Israelite soldier's female prisoner his "captive bride"[21] does not merely neutralize the situation the biblical author describes, it also actively aligns with the author's rape culture discourse. And yet scholars (and spiritual leaders) have used this very text to assert that Israelite law was both advanced and compassionate, claiming, among other things, that it constitutes a kindness because the imprisoned woman was permitted to mourn her family and was spared enslavement.[22]

These are readings that obfuscate and silence truth. Deuteronomy 21:10–14 demonstrates that female captives effectively become slaves to the men who capture them. A man who finds a female prisoner "beautiful to look at" (אשת יפת תאר) and who desires her may bring her into his home, where she must cut her hair, pare her nails, take off her garments and live untouched for a month—most likely to prove that she is not pregnant with another man's child.[23] The Israelite soldier thereafter becomes her master. He is limited in what he can do with her and her body in only one respect: if he tires of his prisoner, he may not sell her as a slave. We must imagine what could possibly happen to a foreign woman discarded by her Israelite master if we are to grasp how grave her condition would be regardless of this one stipulation. Where in Israelite society could she go? How would she sustain herself?[24] Kawashima regards this proviso as some sort of compensation for the fact that the woman's abductor did not negotiate her father's approval when he captured her (13). Perhaps. In wartime, of course, women's fathers are slaughtered, and therefore can be presumed to be unavailable for such parley. Special waivers apply.

When soldiers around the world take women prisoner (many as children, dragged from their schools), when they rape them repeatedly, when they then describe their captive as their "wife," do we not respond with justified, unmitigated rage? In any other context we would hardly dignify what the Hebrew Bible describes in Deuteronomy 21:10–14 by using terms associated with marriage. We might call what this text describes an arranged rape, but certainly not an arranged marriage. If we accept the biblical author's terms for the rights of an Israelite soldier to the women he captured, if we normalize such laws and narratives by the claim that "this is how things were done back then," we might as well accept and normalize the mass rapes of the Yazidi women and girls by ISIS soldiers, or the 2014 kidnapping and forced "marriage" of 276 Nigerian schoolgirls by adherents of Boko Haram. Our present-day rage means nothing if it allows free passes: sexual assault anywhere and everywhere, in any media, in any art or literature, in any society, must be named for what it is. Otherwise, we are compromised before we speak at all. Worse, we collude with ancient texts by excusing and rationalizing their violent content.

There may indeed be no equivalent term for "rape" in the Hebrew Bible. But there are plenty of words used to describe sexual violence perpetrated against both female and male characters. Biblical characters are "molested" (נגע), "taken" (לקח), "seized" (חזק), "laid" (שכב), and "degraded" (ענה). Sexual violence is described with relish: Israel, personified as the deity's wife, is exposed, her clothing stripped from her, her nakedness laid bare to her husband and, not infrequently, his audience (Jer. 13:20–27; Isa. 47:3, Hosea 2:5, Nah. 3:5). Just because there is no specific word for a given rape act does not mean that the idea of the act doesn't exist or that the act has never been committed. As Gwynn Kessler points out, texts like those we find in Deuteronomy 15 and 21 are riddled with what she terms "structural violence," defined by "the very presumption of the texts . . . that people can be bought, sold, and owned, or women can be captured and raped, kept, or discarded, as a matter of course" (2019, 61). And, as Kessler further notes, because such violence is presented to readers in legal and authoritative terms, it is often read passively, accepted without question (ibid.). When scholars simply reprise this presentation without any interrogation or resistance, they are colluding in the perpetuation of its inherent structural violence.

It is not merely a mistake to avoid interrogating the sexual violence of the Hebrew Bible; it is also ethically wrong. Normalizing the text and reproducing the world view of its authors without judgment is to validate authors who are depicting a rape culture as an *ideal* culture, headed by a deity who is himself a perpetrator of sexual violence. If the best we can do is admit that there is a "gap" in the authors' ethical and legal thinking (Kawashima 2011, 21), then we have done far worse than nothing at all. Such a move excuses; it does not analyze. There is no "gap," here. The laws and narratives detailing sexual violence are the logical *outcome* of the kind of thinking that stands behind the Hebrew Bible. Laws that were, until recently, the law of the land in the western world, ones that permitted a man to beat and rape his wife, were produced in the same way. They are not "gaps" in legal thinking but products of the same. We are living, everywhere, in cultures that continue to support sexual violence of all kinds.

The Hebrew Bible is among the most influential collections of texts we can name; it has been carried around the globe and used to support colonialization, oppression, and enslavement. Its texts have served in the exploitation of women and men across the world. Its stories are told and retold, permeating every artistic media we know. Clerics purport to explain their meaning; secular authorities claim to act on their dictates. Scholars who treat the sexual violence in its pages as something to describe in "historical context" contribute to the normalization of the terror done with these texts. The Hebrew Bible has been and continues to be used as an instrument of hate against the LGBTQ+ community. LGBTQ+ individuals have been murdered or driven to suicide by those who use biblical texts to justify their violence.

White Christian men have been the most destructive purveyors of biblical texts in the pursuit of power and domination for centuries. Jews and Romani peoples of Europe have paid a horrific price for that pursuit.[25] People of color around the globe have had their languages, cultures, and communities destroyed to make way for the white man's Bible.[26] Israel, a nation that bases its claims to territory on texts of the Hebrew Bible, has built a system of oppression of Palestinians that has, among its many horrors, included the rape of Palestinian prisoners.[27]

The Bible is often deployed in ways that implicitly and explicitly condone sexual violence against women. After the 1968 Mỹ Lai massacre was described in court—horrors that included rape and mutilation of Vietnamese women and children—an American judge alluded to scripture to justify overturning the murder conviction of platoon leader Lieutenant William L. Calley, Jr.: "Now Joshua did not have charges brought against him for the slaughter of the civilian population of Jericho . . ."²⁸ The Book of Ruth is regularly presented as the quintessential text of communal lovingkindness; the fact that its second chapter describes how Ruth, a migrant woman, faces sexual assault in the fields is simply occluded (Shepherd 2001, *passim*). Religious leaders have used biblical texts in ways that blame rape victims; even today, religious leaders can pick up where Martin Luther (and so many other church authorities) left off, blaming Dinah for her immodesty in "going out" (Gen. 34:1)—an immodesty, it is claimed, that either signaled sexual availability to Shechem or simply invited his aggression (Gen. 34:2; see Schroeder 1997, *passim*). Then, there is the simple strategy of bypassing: Deuteronomy 21:10–14, which describes how Israelite men may take captive women in war and rape them until they tire of them, does not serve as a topic for discussion in the pews despite obvious parallels in our own time.

Biblical texts are taught in religious schools. They are the stuff of popular culture. Biblical sexual violence ignored or valorized by religious traditions—and by the cultures that export their stories in multiple venues—legitimates today's rape culture. Biblical texts tell stories of patriarchal systems, genocide, enslavement, and rape; left uninterrogated, they serve as central pillars of rape culture. David's military prowess is a quintessential example. He is a hero, a tender poet, and a valiant warrior whose mutilation of his enemies, indecent exposure, and "taking" of wives and concubines is ignored, tolerated, or excused. In valorizing male power and accepting male aggression in biblical texts, we do not simply condone rape cultures, we help perpetuate them.

Scholars, then, must not treat the Hebrew Bible as a "mere" artifact of the past. They have an ethical obligation to strip away any protections granted under the guise of scientific objectivity. It is likely that these texts have more impact, more importance, and more power to affect the lives of human beings in our time than they did in ancient Israel—after all, they are now considered sacred and authoritative texts across the entire globe. The Hebrew Bible is not a museum piece. It is a prooftext for religious and secular cultures alike. It is a tool for training religious leaders, for the instruction and indoctrination of the faithful, and for dissemination of foundational cultural narratives to secular audiences everywhere. Its effects on the material lives of human beings are beyond measure.

Exploring the Text: Aims and Approach

Rape in the House of David: A Company of Men interrogates the ways that male characters in the Books of Samuel freely use the language of sexual violence and liberally engage in enacting it. Again: an Israelite king will sexually humiliate his wife before a court filled with male retainers. An Israelite general will engage in sexualized violence against his enemies on a grand scale, cutting off their foreskins, slicing off their heads or limbs, and using their swords and spears to penetrate and feminize them. Women will be sexually assaulted in word and deed, raped, gang raped, and butchered in the pursuit of male honor and male power. If, as philosopher J.M. Bernstein writes, "ideas of human worth, however sustained as components of a belief system, have been realized and made actual only through the social practices of the peoples concerned" (2015, 138), then we can say that the Hebrew Bible reveals a world in which human worth is often defined by men's ability to commit sexual violence of all kinds. Such a man is esteemed. He has earned the right to become king of Israel.

We must, therefore, understand the full range of semantic possibilities and metaphors for sexual violence that are deployed by biblical authors. We must examine where sexually violent language constitutes an assault against male or female characters. We need to assess every act of sexual violence we find. These undergird the power structures of the Hebrew Bible—a text regarded as authoritative and even sacrosanct across the world.

Two caveats. First, there is no final reading. The Hebrew Bible has been interpreted for millennia, and for good reason. Its language is polyvalent, open to multiple interpretations, and, at times, downright mystifying. My reading rests on the labor of scholars in feminist studies, queer studies, and masculinity studies. My own hope is to make a contribution to our shared concerns. While I argue for my own reading with all the tools I have at hand and all the conviction I feel, I do not presume that my work provides the last word on the subject at hand. There is no final conclusion to the work of my guild, and our readings offer us multiple truths about these texts. Second, any assumption that the diverse texts included in the Hebrew Bible constitute a unified statement on rape, even in just one "ancient context," is flawed. They don't and they can't; these are texts produced over many centuries by multiple authors and editors. We are dealing with authors who assume that their audience understands their language in the time and the region in which they are writing. Those audiences, times, and regions vary considerably.

Still, for all the many things we don't know, we know that the Hebrew Bible is a collection of texts produced and assembled by an elite group of men. We may not know the individual authors, but we do know that they are almost certainly all male, all advantaged, and that the world they portray was dominated by male concerns. Given that these texts were edited and redacted an unknown number of times, any notion of a singular author is rendered meaningless. Nevertheless, we can analyze the texts for what they may reveal about a shared *Weltanschauung* (world view). Cheryl Exum has it right when she describes the biblical narrator as "a collective androcentric unconscious" (2016, 121).

The "collective androcentric unconscious" is at work in the narrative that tells us how David rose to power and how he and his sons exercised that power, despite the fact that the narrative is the product of different authors and its strands are interwoven and redacted. It is true: scholars can identify different political agendas at work in interwoven texts. Readers will find one story told twice or even three times. There are gaps in the text, and Hebrew terms that bear multiple or ambiguous meanings. The Hebrew Bible makes for cryptic, even confusing, reading. Much here is challenging to understand, and scholars will likely continue debating the "actual" meaning of given texts and terms.[29]

Nevertheless, biblical authors share important premises about how their stories should be told, what values undergird their telling, and which characters should be valorized and what they should be valorized for. There is, indeed, an identifiable conceptual framework around male power and the male social order that pervades the stories of Saul, of David, and of the whole company of men we will meet.[30]

Biblical authors build narratives around men striving for power in an honor-based society. Male characters are challenged, defeated, and forced to change or to adjust. No male, not even the deity, is exempt from finding his power contested. Rank is earned, lost, and reclaimed. Kings weaken and die; princes who believe they have deposed their fathers will themselves be slain in humiliating circumstances. Those challenges exist, however, not to lead us to question the right of male characters to their rank and power, but rather to reveal what makes an ideal man (and king) ideal in the first place. If subversion is everywhere, then so is victory. However ephemeral triumph may be, winning reveals the model that both biblical authors and their audience are expected to applaud. The restoration of the male order is the goal and outcome.

Unsurprisingly, war and sex are linked, men and women function largely as binary oppositions, and men who appear to act like women are unmanned, denigrated, and doomed to die some version of social death. The Hebrew term for "hand" or "penis" (יד) is used, as so many have noted, both to refer to military might and the male member (Ex. 13:3, Isa. 10:32, Isa. 57:8). Texts in 1 Samuel about David and Jonathan's presumed mutual love and affection demonstrate that the latter has to play the wife to the former, and in so doing, he loses his right to the throne.[31] Men are not only entitled to perform any act of violence that assures them power, *they have to do so* if their aim is to rule. No restrictions apply.[32]

To rule, in the Hebrew Bible, requires a willing embrace of sexual violence. It also requires the support of other men. Biblical rape culture is supported by male friendships, alliances, and shared homosocial experience. This is not merely a biblical phenomenon, either. In our time, at least one in every five rapes, and possibly as many as one in every three, is a gang rape (see Da Silva, Harkins, and Woodhams 2013, 15–16).[33] *Frontline*, America's Public Broadcasting Station (PBS) documentary program, has produced documentaries on rape culture in night shift and agricultural work settings, where men create working conditions that render immigrant women vulnerable to sexual violence.[34] Women across the world have been announcing "me too," demonstrating that acts of sexual harassment and violence are depressingly common. Such acts are committed with the collusion and cooperation of men.[35] As soon as we name the events that prove how pernicious male collaboration is when it comes to acts of sexual violence, our naming is outpaced. Tomorrow will bring more of the same.

In the Hebrew Bible, servants, counselors, generals, and friends help make rape possible and work to protect its perpetrators. We lack, however, focused attention on the company of men engaged in supporting sexual violence. Such companies of men appear in every rape narrative we find in the Books of Samuel. They even include the deity, Yhwh. This book therefore goes beyond the study of the Bible's individual acts of rape and their immediate political aftermath to focus on the web of relationships that makes such acts possible. In the following chapters, I argue that the Hebrew Bible's rape culture is both generated and maintained by male competitions for rank and power and by alliances and friendships that sustain male authority and control.

I have deliberately chosen not to present my material "chronologically." Instead, I organize according to type and theme. In Chapter 1, "Disposing of Daughters, Sisters, and Wives: The Rapes of Tamar and of David's *Pilagshim*," I begin with examples of rape that generally go undisputed. Amnon's rape of Tamar will be our starting point. We will see that this rape involves not just one perpetrator but a company of men who collude in its enactment. The men who play a role are not limited to central actors; supporting figures are just as critical to the humiliation, degradation, and destruction of Tamar. Her rape is a public event, not a private one. This chapter also examines Absalom's rape of David's *pilagshim*, a mass rape that likewise features a public humiliation of its victims. Though committed by one man, these rapes, too, are imagined by men, witnessed by men, and supported by men.

In the second chapter, "The Taking, Trapping, and Raping of Women: Michal and Bathsheba," I discuss the way male characters in the Books of Samuel procure women for their sexual use. The sexual violence at work in the narratives of Michal and Bathsheba is often downplayed, and the collusion of a host of men in this violence is left un(der)examined. The bodies of both women are used in competitions for power among dominant males. Less powerful men ingratiate themselves by helping their leaders gain sexual access to women's bodies and by facilitating their exhibitionist displays. In so doing, they participate vicariously in what those leaders do.

In the third and final chapter, "The Once and the Future King: Saul, David, and the Practice of Sexual Violence," I explore how the language and metaphors of sexual violence saturate the narrative, frequently demonstrating how women can be raped by proxy and men can (and should) rape their enemies. We discover that the best king for Israel is the one who is most invested in and adept at the use of sexual violence. This last chapter should make it abundantly clear: the Books of Samuel present a rape culture that permeates every aspect of the world they describe.

Who Wrote This Book? On the Need for Authorial Transparency

Decades ago, when I trained as a historian, I was taught to assume a particular persona. My research was expected to produce data that others could check and verify; my purpose was to maintain appropriate distance and avoid emotional investment. Those who would read my work did not need to know anything about me or my history; such things were irrelevant and unimportant, a distraction I should avoid provoking if I wanted to be taken seriously.

I still believe that my research should produce data others can check, validate, or, indeed, attempt to refute. I no longer believe, however, that I should pretend to some kind of anonymity. I have a history which has formed me and agendas that motivate me. This, then, is data you are welcome to: I was born to a middle-class white family in America's Midwest, affording me enormous advantages from birth. I was fed and schooled. I am an aging feminist, a cisgender and heterosexual woman whose parents were themselves college graduates. I am, therefore, privileged in many regards.

I was born and raised a Jew in a world controlled by Christians. It still is, of course, and that is not an insignificant fact for me. Christians have for millennia deployed the Hebrew Bible to dismiss, degrade, and demonize Jews; I am well versed in that history as a teacher of the formation and development of European anti-Judaism and antisemitism. I worry that my own critique of the Hebrew Bible could be used to reinforce such traditions. And yet . . .

During the writing of this book, I heard from colleagues and students who were dealing with toxic environments marked by male entitlement and male privilege. Perpetrators of sexual harassment and sexual violence are experts at maintaining plausible deniability when their actions provoke scrutiny. In fact, they are rarely questioned in the first place; victims have reason to remain silent in a world that typically shames and punishes them for speaking out. I have no female colleague I know well who has not herself experienced or witnessed sexual harassment; I can count myself among them, and my own experience spans multiple educational settings and many decades. I also have few female colleagues who have not experienced sexual assault, and I am well aware that the number of my students—regardless of gender—who have endured sexual harassment and sexual violence is an outrage. To work towards attaining "distance" on these realities is, in my view, heartless.

As an ordained rabbi, I am cognizant of the value placed on the Hebrew Bible and the damage spiritual leaders do in downplaying or bypassing the violence in its texts. As an academic and a teacher, I know that global cultures have been permeated by biblical narratives whose violence has been ignored, justified, and even romanticized. In my view, sexual harassment, abuse, and assault remain stark realities in every country on our planet. We must continue to sound the alarm. Silence shames, intimidates, and erases victims.

It is the measure of a rape culture that it thrives on abuse. Harassment and intimidation are par for the course. Sexual violence and rape are ubiquitous. Rape cultures sustain colonialism and cement disparities in race, class, and gender, globally. They control and police sexual behavior. They punish non-heteronormative sexual expression. Their reach is as broad as the systems of power that maintain them. Many of my colleagues in both secular and denominational realms teach biblical texts. If they (and I) cannot name the rape culture we see in texts of the Hebrew Bible, we remain blind to the rape cultures of our own time. To that end, then, this work.

Notes

1 Of 15,000 publicly available deepfakes analyzed in one study, some 96% were of women (Dunn 2020, 12).
2 They have been hunted and threatened with sexual assault, and shot. See Dunn, *passim,* for an overview.
3 The Abu Ghraib prison, located in Abu Ghraib, Iraq, opened in the 1950s. The U.S. used the prison between 2003 and 2006; reports of the torture and sexual humiliation of Iraqi detainees emerged in 2004. See www.newyorker.com/magazine/2004/05/10/torture-at-abu-ghraib.
4 Statistics on sexual violence against transgender and non-binary individuals are underreported, given the number of countries where such individuals live, essentially, in hiding. For statistics in the United States, see www.nsvrc.org/sites/default/files/publications/2019-02/Transgender_infographic_508_0.pdf.

5 See, for example, www.ijm.org/our-work/sexual-violence-against-children. For a review of literature on sexual violence against the elderly, see Bows 2017, *passim*.
6 Using the definitive article *the* before the term "Hebrew Bible" is problematic; what we refer to as "the Hebrew Bible" is *an* assemblage of texts deemed authoritative. There are other versions of this anthology. For a brief discussion, see Thiede 2022, 1–2.
7 See also Hosea 2:12–13.
8 Scholz argues that Samson is also threatened with rape (2017, 178).
9 For a discussion of the sexual and rape imagery in this text, see Guest 2006, 169–74.
10 Many scholars suggest that Yael is enacting a "reverse rape." See Guest 2011, 23; Bal 1988, 21; Bledstein 1993, 41; Yee 1993, 116; van Wolde 1995, 245; Haddox 2013, 79; Graybill 2018, 197.
11 Niditch (2008) relies on Emily Vermeule's *Aspects of Death in Early Greek Art and Poetry* (1979, 101–3).
12 The term *pilegesh* (plural, *pilagshim*) is problematic. "Concubine" is anachronistic. A *pilegesh* is not understood as a full or first wife and might be termed a "secondary wife." I shall rely, throughout this book, on transliteration for this Hebrew term in order to avoid evoking associations with the term "concubine" and the awkwardness of "secondary wife."
13 The term "rape culture" emerged from second-wave feminism's work exposing the prevalence of rape as a feature of life for women in the 1970s. The pervasive nature of sexual violence against cisgender heterosexual and homosexual men, trans, and non-binary individuals suggests that the term should include the systemic nature of sexual violence of all kinds.
14 I explore this theme in my book *Male Friendship, Homosociality, and Women of the Hebrew Bible: Malignant Fraternities* (2022, *passim*).
15 Scholars advocating the use of these categories argue that they apply to biblical texts and are essential for addressing sexual violence in our own time. See Graybill, Minister, and Lawrence 2019, 12–13.
16 See Leviticus 19:20–22 for additional legislation on the use of a woman's body.
17 Some scholars note that Rebekah's family asks her if she wants to marry Isaac (Gen. 24:58–9). This is a singular exception to the rule. Women are otherwise "taken" by men in the Hebrew Bible. They are not asked for permission or consent.
18 It is telling that the word "forcible" is used here.
19 As we see when men insist that "no" means "yes." See, for example, archive. thinkprogress.org/fraternity-loses-its-charter-after-displaying-no-means-yes-banner-at-a-party-9a7522f1181c/ and www.cosmopolitan.com/politics/news/a8886/yale-fraternity-dke-rape-chant/. As Rhiannon Graybill writes, consent is, as such, a fuzzy concept (2021, 30–31).
20 Washington notes that biblical "rape laws" regulate sexual assault: "The laws do not interdict sexual violence; rather they stipulate the terms under which a man may commit rape" (1998, 211).
21 Some scholars suggest that biblical texts describe customs involving the capture of women for the purposes of marriage. Niditch suggests that Judges 21, which describes the abduction of young women of Shiloh, "may well be an etiology for

customs involving marriage—a yearly 'wife stealing' ritual in which matches are made between men of Benjamin and daughters of Shiloh" (2008, 210). Katherine Southwood (2017) has made similar arguments, arguing that since there is no exact word in Hebrew for "rape," one should be leery of using it (e.g., 16, 116, 119, 148, 155, 165, 233).

22 Washington surveys scholars who excuse and even valorize this text (1998, 202–7). In *Not in Heaven: The Nature and Function of Halakha*, Eliezer Berkovits writes that "by ordering the soldier who desired a female captive to take her for a wife, the Torah was educating people toward humane behavior" (1983, 13). This text is still taught in progressive Jewish seminaries to rabbinic students.

23 See also Judges 21:20–23, where the Benjaminites, advised to capture young women celebrating a festival to Yhwh, lie in wait until the women are out in the open and take them prisoner, forcing them into becoming their wives and bearing their children.

24 M.I. Rey discusses the ethnic and racial dimensions of this law (2016, *passim*).

25 For a brief bibliography of studies on Christian complicity in the murder of European Jews, see www.ushmm.org/collections/bibliography/christianity-and-the-holocaust. For a brief survey of Christian involvement in the destruction of Romani peoples, see encyclopedia.ushmm.org/content/en/article/genocide-of-european-roma-gypsies-1939-1945.

26 An introductory bibliography on Christian complicity in apartheid, for example, can be found here: people.ucalgary.ca/~nurelweb/papers/irving/apart.html. For a discussion of how the Bible was received, then used to resist colonial efforts, see West 2016, *passim*.

27 Weishut 2015, *passim*.

28 Quoted in Washington 1998, 324.

29 For example, James Harding's discussion of the Hebrew word translated as "love," *ahava* (אהבה), extends over seven pages (2013, 73–80).

30 Blurring of categories occurs in biblical texts, whether these appear in languaging a female with male terms (e.g., Rebekah in Gen. 24) or in dressing a man in what might normally be understood to be female garb (e.g., Moses with a veil). Biblical representations sometimes counter ideals of male dominance. Subverting and queering these texts is vital for the mental health of real human beings, whose sexuality and gender cannot be categorized along a neat binary.

31 As I argue in chapter 2 of *Male Friendship, Homosociality, and Women in the Hebrew Bible: Malignant Fraternities*, 37–62.

32 The biblical audience understood the rape of the Levite's *pilegesh* as wrong because it insulted Yhwh and his holy elite guardsman, his Levite, not because of the violence she endured. See Thiede 2022, 110–33.

33 Gang rapes are less often reported than are rapes by a single perpetrator. See Da Silva, Harkins, and Woodhams 2013, 14–15.

34 See www.pbs.org/wgbh/frontline/film/rape-in-the-fields/ and www.pbs.org/wgbh/frontline/film/rape-on-the-night-shift/.

35 And women, sometimes, too. At the time of this writing, a jury found Ghislaine Maxwell guilty on five of six counts related to her facilitation of Jeffrey Epstein's sexual abuse of minors between 1994 and 2004. Those counts included sex trafficking of a minor, transporting a minor with the intent to engage in criminal sexual activity, and three related counts of conspiracy.

Bibliography

Abasili, Alexander Izuchukwu. "Was It Rape? The David and Bathsheba Pericope Re-Examined." *Vetus Testamentum* 61, no. 1 (January 1, 2011): 1–15. doi:10.1163/156853311X548596.

Bal, Mieke. *Death & Dissymmetry: The Politics of Coherence in the Book of Judges*. Chicago: The University of Chicago Press, 1988.

Berkovits, Eliezer. *Not in Heaven: The Nature and Function of Halakha*. New York: Ktav, 1983.

Bernstein, J.M. *Torture and Dignity: An Essay on Moral Injury*. Chicago: The University of Chicago Press, 2015. doi:10.7208/Chicago/9780226266466.001.0001.

Bledstein, Adrien Janis. "Is Judges a Woman's Satire of Men Who Play God?" In *A Feminist Companion to Judges*, edited by Athalya Brenner, 34–54. Feminist Companion to the Bible 4. Sheffield: Sheffield Academic, 1993.

Bows, Hannah. "Sexual Violence Against Older People: A Review of the Empirical Literature." *Trauma, Violence, & Abuse* 19, no. 5 (January 2, 2017): 567–83. doi:10.1177/1524838016683455.

Da Silva, Teresa, Leigh Harkins, and Jessica Woodhams. "Multiple Perpetrator Rape: An International Phenomenon." In *Handbook on the Study of Multiple Perpetrator Rape: A Multidisciplinary Response to an International Problem*, edited by Miranda A.H. Horvath and Jessica Woodhams, 10–36. London and New York: Routledge, 2013.

Dunn, Suzie. "Forms of TFGBV." In *Technology-Facilitated Gender-Based Violence: An Overview*, edited by Suzie Dunn, 5–16. Centre for International Governance Innovation, January 1, 2020. Accessed June 12, 2021. www.jstor.org/stable/resrep27513.10.

Exum, J. Cheryl. *Fragmented Women: Feminist (Sub)versions of Biblical Narratives*, 2nd ed. Cornerstones Series. London: Bloomsbury T&T Clark, 2016.

Graybill, Rhiannon. "Day of the Woman: Judges 4–5 as Slasher and Rape Revenge Narrative." *The Journal of Religion and Popular Culture* 30, no. 3 (Fall 2018): 193–205. doi:10.3138/jrpc.2017-0016.

Graybill, Rhiannon. *Texts of Terror: Rape, Sexual Violence, & the Hebrew Bible*. New York: Oxford University Press, 2021.

Graybill, Rhiannon, Meredith Minister, and Beatrice Lawrence. "Introduction." In *Rape Culture and Religious Studies: Critical and Pedagogical Engagements*, edited by Rhiannon Graybill, Meredith Minister, and Beatrice Lawrence, 1–20. Feminist Studies and Sacred Texts 1. London: Lexington, 2019.

Guest, Deryn. "Judges." In *The Queer Bible Commentary*, edited by Deryn Guest, Robert E. Goss, Mona West, and Thomas Bohache, 167–89. London: SCM Press, 2006.

Guest, Deryn. "From Gender Reversal to Genderfuck: Reading Jael Through a Lesbian Lens." In *Bible Trouble: Queer Reading at the Boundaries of Biblical Scholarship*, edited by Teresa J. Hornsby and Ken Stone, 9–43. Semeia Studies 67. Atlanta: Society of Biblical Literature, 2011.

Haddox, Susan. "Gendering Violence and Violating Gender in Judges 4–5." *Conversations with the Biblical World* 33 (2013): 67–81.

Harding, James E. *The Love of David and Jonathan: Ideology, Text, Reception*. Sheffield: Equinox, 2013.

Kawashima, Robert S. "Could a Woman Say 'No' in Biblical Israel? On the Genealogy of Legal Status in Biblical Law and Literature." *AJS Review* 35, no. 1 (April 2011): 1–22.

Kessler, Gwynn. "Teaching Rape, Slavery, and Genocide in Bible and Culture." In *Rape Culture and Religious Studies: Critical and Pedagogical Engagements*, edited by Rhiannon Graybill, Meredith Minister, and Beatrice Lawrence, 1–20. Feminist Studies and Sacred Texts 1. London: Lexington, 2019.

Lipka, Hilary. *Sexual Transgression in the Hebrew Bible*. Sheffield: Phoenix Press, 2006.

Nagouse, Emma. "'To Ransom a Man's Soul': Male Rape and Gender Identity in *Outlander* and 'The Suffering Man' of Lamentations 3." In *Rape Culture, Gender Violence and Religion: Biblical Perspectives*, edited by Caroline Blyth, Emily Colgan, and Katie B. Edwards, 143–58. Cham, Switzerland: Palgrave Macmillan, 2018. doi:10.1007/978-3-319-70669-6_9.

Niditch, Susan. *Judges: A Commentary*. The Old Testament Library. Louisville: Westminster John Knox Press, 2008.

Rey, M.I. "Reexamination of the Foreign Female Captive: Deuteronomy 21:10–14 as a Case of Genocidal Rape." *Journal of Feminist Studies in Religion* 32, no. 1 (Spring 2016): 37–53.

Scholz, Susanne. *The Bible as Political Artifact: On the Feminist Study of the Hebrew Bible*. Minneapolis: Fortress Press, 2017.

Scholz, Susanne. "Reading Biblical Texts Beyond a Cop-Out Hermeneutics in the Trump Era." In *Rape Culture and Religious Studies: Critical and Pedagogical Engagements*, edited by Rhiannon Graybill, Meredith Minister, and Beatrice Lawrence, 1–20. Feminist Studies and Sacred Texts 1. London: Lexington, 2019.

Schroeder, Joy A. "The Rape of Dinah: Luther's Interpretation of a Biblical Narrative." *The Sixteenth Century Journal* 28, no. 3 (Autumn 1997): 775–91. doi:10.2307/2542991.

Schulte, Leah Rediger. *The Absence of God in Biblical Rape Narratives*. Minneapolis: Fortress Press, 2017.

Shepherd, David. "Violence in the Fields? Translating, Reading, and Revising in Ruth 2." *The Catholic Biblical Quarterly* 63, no. 3 (July 2001): 444–63.

Southwood, Katherine E. *Marriage by Capture in the Book of Judges: An Anthropological Approach*. New York: Cambridge University Press, 2017.

Thiede, Barbara. *Male Friendship, Homosociality, and Women of the Hebrew Bible: Malignant Fraternities*. Routledge Studies in the Biblical World 5. London and New York: Routledge, 2022. doi:10.4324/9780429326226.

van Wolde, Ellen J. "Ya'el in Judges 4." *Zeitschrift für die alttestamentliche Wissenschaft* 107, no. 2 (1995): 240–46. doi:10.1515/zatw.1995.107.2.240.

Vermeule, Emily. *Aspects of Death in Early Greek Art and Poetry*. Sather Classical Lectures 46. Berkeley: University of California Press, 1979. doi:10.1525/9780520310827.

Washington, Harold C. "'Lest He Die in the Battle and Another Man Take Her': Violence and the Construction of Gender in the Laws of Deuteronomy 20–22." In

Gender and Law in the Hebrew Bible and the Ancient Near East, edited by Victor H. Matthews, Tivka Frymer-Kensky, and Bernard M. Levinson, 185–213. Sheffield: Sheffield Academic Press, 1998.

Weishut, Daniel J.N. "Sexual Torture of Palestinian Men by Israeli Authorities." *Reproductive Health Matters* 23, no. 46 (2015): 71–84. doi:10.1016/j.rhm.2015.11.019.

West, Gerald O. *The Stolen Bible: From Tool of Imperialism to African Icon*. Leiden, The Netherlands and Pietermaritzburg, South Africa: Brill and Cluster Publications, 2016.

Yee, Gale A. "By the Hand of a Woman: The Metaphor of the Woman Warrior in Judges 4." *Semeia: An Experimental Journal for Biblical Criticism* 61 (1993): 99–132.

1 Disposing of Daughters, Sisters, and Wives

The Rapes of Tamar and of David's *Pilagshim*

Introduction: The Ideal Man, Hegemonic Masculinity, and Biblical Rape Culture

The ideal man of the Hebrew Bible is a warrior well-endowed in looks and strength. He is an effective and persuasive speaker, ready and willing to bond with the men who support him and ally with him. He is effectively "womanless," even as he collects women and their bodies to attest to his prowess and produce offspring (Clines 2009, 216–27).[1]

In the Books of Samuel, the ideal man is someone who often engages in sexual violence. He takes women and he rapes them. He symbolically rapes men too. Sexual violence is an essential instrument for sustaining his command over other men and for performing biblical standards of model masculinity. Lesser men may become partners, bystanders, or witnesses to the sexual violence practiced by men in charge. By colluding, cooperating, and acquiescing in sexual violence, they confirm that they, too, belong to and uphold the male homosocial order.

Male characters in the Hebrew Bible, regardless of rank, belong to a system of biblical hegemonic masculinity. Hegemonic masculinity works to establish male domination and female subordination (Connell 2005, 77). It is maintained through zero-sum struggles for status and control. Even the men who lose in the battles over position, authority, and honor will not disavow the premises of the contest, but rather hope (and strive) to win the next time around. The competition is relentless; masculinity must be continually performed and repeatedly proven. As such, masculinity is inherently unstable. Still, male biblical authors describe failures for a purpose: the audience learns who fails at masculinity in order to understand what it takes to succeed.

Because hierarchies of dominance are often worked out through sexual violence in the Hebrew Bible, the ideal king must, perforce, be capable of rape. Rape is a medium for challenges to his supremacy. Thus, though

DOI: 10.4324/9781003014911-2

2 Samuel 13 is so often called "The Rape of Tamar," the sexual violence in this text is a tool, not the topic: a conduit for men to challenge one another's honor and power.[2] The rape of David's *pilagshim* (2 Sam. 16:22)[3] is likewise not about the women themselves but is rather part of a battle for sovereignty and the throne.[4] When sexual violence is the means by which power in the narrative is negotiated, rape becomes the inevitable language of the text.[5]

In these biblical books, when women are raped, murder will follow. Rape either establishes or escalates conflicts between men; it is an intermediary step that leads to the death of the enemy, one that is often itself sexualized and violent. David takes and rapes Bathsheba and has her husband Uriah murdered. Amnon rapes Tamar and is murdered by Absalom. Absalom rapes his father's *pilagshim* and is in turn murdered by David's right-hand man and nephew, Joab. The arc of the story is about men, not about women. What matters is which man wins and which man loses, who lives and who dies. Sexual violence against women is part of the author's literary inventory, an established vehicle for showing how male rivalries unfold.

Rape in the Hebrew Bible does not typically feature multiple perpetrators. Multiple colluders, bystanders, and witnesses are another matter. In these narratives, men indulge in sharing women's bodies, both in word and deed. Together they ogle women and partner in trapping women for their sexual use. They evoke the act of rape with other men, sharing mental images of the woman's body made accessible to them well before the actual act is committed. Men actively plan rape with other men. They rape within earshot of other men and rape in front of other men. They rape their own sisters; and they rape the daughters, sisters, and wives of other men.

Voyeurism is integral to the experience. The Hebrew Bible's rapists make it possible for other men not merely to imagine the violation of women, but to know it will occur, to listen in, and sometimes to watch. When men share sex talk, sex images, and sex acts, when they invite each other to participate in the use of a woman's body, they bond.[6] A lesser man may not be able to rape as the ideal man can, but he can vicariously experience the act, witness it as a bystander, or help bring it about. Someday, *he* might be the man to invite others to the party.

In a rape culture, no man rapes alone. He has an entire system behind him to support and applaud what he does, excuse what he does, or condone what he does. In the Hebrew Bible too, male alliances, friendships, and relationships underpin sexual assault. This chapter addresses the male networks that produce the rapes of David's daughter Tamar and his *pilagshim*. These rapes are connected, part of a larger trajectory in which sexual violence regularly serves as a means for negotiating power among men. David and his sons all possess influence and authority. In the exercise of their authority, they will imagine rape, enable rape, and become rapists themselves.

Kinship relations are critical to biblical systems of male dominance. In David's house, fathers, sons, and brothers use the bodies of women to compete, contest, and challenge one another. Amnon seeks to use Tamar's body in order to humiliate and challenge Absalom, his rival for the throne. Absalom rapes his father's *pilagshim* to symbolically emasculate his father. And Adonijah makes an attempt to acquire David's former servant, the beautiful virgin Abishag and, in so doing, seals his death warrant at Solomon's hands. David and his sons establish their rank, status, and dominion through obtaining sexual access to women and through using sexual violence against them.

Family relationships do not exist isolated from the systems they inhabit. Male friendships and alliances in the Hebrew Bible depend on women's bodies not merely for their expression, but for their very creation.[7] In the Books of Samuel, friends and counselors will play critical roles in suggesting, planning, and colluding in rape; male alliances will be cemented, even forged, through sexual violence. There will be other men who are drawn into the planning and the witnessing. Attendants, courtiers, soldiers—all these will be present at the crime. There will be much display of sexual violence, and there will be consumption of the spectacle by both the male characters and the biblical audiences for each tale. Even the modern reader must assume the role of voyeur.

Biblical authors care about depicting sexual violence as a tool, not as a crime. The victims are unimportant. Tamar and the *pilagshim* may survive their rapes, but only as living ghosts who rapidly disappear from the pages of the Hebrew Bible. They can serve no future purpose because they are significant only as the conduits for male competition. Once they are sexually used, they are discarded by the men in the narrative, and by the biblical authors too.

2 Samuel 13: The Rape of Tamar

It takes just six verses to discover how many men in David's family will play a role in the rape of Tamar. The princess is introduced as Absalom's beautiful sister (2 Sam. 13:1).[8] In the next verse, Tamar's half-brother Amnon is brought on stage—sick "because of his sister" and tormented because it is impossible for him to "do anything to her" (לעשות לה מאומה). Tamar is not only Absalom's sister, she is also a virgin (13:2).[9] Next, the author introduces the man who will solve Amnon's dilemma: Jonadab, son of David's brother Shimah, nephew to the king and friend and cousin to the heir. Jonadab immediately provides Amnon with a plan that relies on drawing in yet another member of the family, the one presumably most responsible for protecting sexual access to Tamar: her father, King David.

The princess has no identity and no purpose outside of her relationship to each of these men. Instructed by Joab, Amnon asks the king, "Let my sister Tamar come" (2 Sam. 13:6). In turn, David sends a message that similarly defines his daughter: "Please go to the house of your brother Amnon" (13:7). Even Absalom, who strangely manages to turn up almost immediately after Tamar is raped (13:20), makes clear that his sister is only important in terms of the men she is related to. As she stands before him with ashes on her head and her garment rent, he asks: "has your brother been with you?" (האמינון אחיך היה עמך).[10]

Sexual access to a family's women is guarded by men who use it to secure or advance their own interests.[11] One should presume that Tamar's virginity would be protected by both her father, the king, and her brothers. Her movements are their charge (Matthews and Benjamin 1997, 344–45). But just as there are reasons to protect sexual access to the bodies of the women of the family for male purposes, we will see that there can also be reasons to grant their bodies to other men to further male agendas. The goal is to gain and maintain authority and to demonstrate who possesses power and control.

All of these men have official positions, whether as king, prince, or counselor. David's nephew Jonadab is called Amnon's "friend." The term deployed here, *re'a* (רע), is used in royal contexts to refer to a kind of counselor, a "king's friend," whose role is to facilitate marriage alliances (van Selms 1957, 120–22; Bakon 2015, 105).[12] Jonadab is important at court, a counselor and advisor to the heir to David's throne. His family bona fides are given, and his official position vis-à-vis the prince is identified (2 Sam. 13:3). He is, the biblical author also tells us, very shrewd (חכם מאד), "an exceedingly worldly man," as Saul Olyan puts it (2017, 82).

Certainly, Jonadab seems well prepared to deal with Amnon's desires. He immediately provides his cousin with a script. First, Amnon should lie down and pretend to be ill. Then,

> [w]hen your father comes to see you, say to him, "Let my sister Tamar come and give me something to eat. Let her prepare the food in front of me, so that I may look on, and let her serve it to me."
>
> (13:5)

Jonadab evokes what Amnon has already imagined. Tamar, sister of a formidable rival, in *his* rooms, serving *him*, on display for *his* enjoyment. The two men are sharing sex talk, experiencing a fantasy together. It is a bonding moment.

Amnon must, however, find a way to convince his father, the king, to dispatch Tamar to his rooms.[13] Fortunately for the prince, Jonadab knows how to manipulate David. David's son by Bathsheba has just died.[14] A sick and bedridden heir is cause for royal alarm. Jonadab can make use of David's concern. Amnon should ask the king for someone the prince can trust to prepare his food—before his very eyes, no less (2 Sam. 13:5). Such a request implies that Amnon's food has been tampered with or might be while he is (presumably) helpless and sick. Tamar is his sister. She can be trusted to prepare food Amnon can eat safely.

Wordplay around just what Tamar should be preparing for her half-brother is part of an unsettling, heavily sexualized interchange among the family's men. When Jonadab suggests how Amnon should articulate his request that Tamar come to prepare food for him (2 Sam. 13:5), his wording features a causative form for "to eat" followed by the word *lechem*, "food" (ותברני לחם). A provocative double entendre is at work. *Lechem* can refer either to food or to a woman.[15] Tamar should come to Amnon's room so that she can *cause him to eat food/woman* (ותברני לחם). The victim becomes the enticer in male fantasies, both then as now.

In that same verse, Jonadab suggests the kind of food Tamar should make for her cousin: *biryah* (בריה). *Biryah* is the sort of food one gives to a person who is sick.[16] But when David arrives, Amnon asks that Tamar make heart cakes for him (לבבות), a kind of pastry that lovers might share (van Dijk-Hemmes 1989, 141). Amnon repeats part of Jonadab's script verbatim in 2 Samuel 13:6, however, explicitly insisting that Tamar should make the cakes before his own eyes (לעיני). In the same verse, he tells the king that Tamar should bring the pastries directly to him so that he can eat the pastries "from her hand" (ואברה מידה).

The text is polyvalent. Amnon could be implying that he needs to watch Tamar in order to make sure the food is safe to eat. And his choice of delicacies reminds the biblical audience that Amnon wants to watch his beautiful sister prepare a tasty treat and feed it to him with her own hands. A woman preparing food as a prelude to sex is a well-known trope. Given the regular association of food and sex in the Hebrew Bible (Stone 2005, *passim*), we can assume that a male biblical audience would make the obvious connections. They would likely assume David does too.

The biblical audience has already experienced Jonadab and Amnon fantasizing about sex with Tamar. The text makes it possible for the audience to imagine the king as part of the male fraternity at work. Amnon's language, after all, suggests that sexual access to Tamar is what he really wants, not her skills as either cook or nurse.[17] Given the sexual overtones, the audience could hardly expect the king to be either ignorant or innocent of Amnon's desires. And David is quite familiar with the relationship of food and sex. He himself deployed one as an inducement for the other in 2 Samuel 11, when he plied Uriah with food and wine to induce him to sleep with the pregnant Bathsheba (Thiede 2022, 69–70).

David sends for Tamar. His messenger tells Tamar that she is to make *biryah*, not heart cakes, for Amnon. David's language ensures that she receive what appears to be an entirely harmless request: her half-brother is ill, and she is asked to nurse him to health.[18] All the male characters may either suspect or share knowledge of the actual motivation for requesting her attention. Tamar should not. The male biblical audience, like the male characters, knows better.[19]

Possibly, David's famed rhetorical abilities are at work, permitting the king to ensure no opprobrium will be cast his way.[20] David is highly skilled in manipulating those who might challenge him. On two occasions, David manipulates circumstances to cast himself as the loyal and pious hero who refuses to take an opportunity to kill the maddened king Saul, who unjustly pursues him.[21] In any case, Tamar is clearly not important to David. Tamar should go to Amnon's rooms; the king has so ordered. Amnon has succeeded in enlisting the king's help. By granting Amnon's request, David enables him.

Kings must watch their backs where their sons are concerned, as David well knows.[22] After Amnon rapes Tamar, David hears of "all the things" (כל הדברים) that have happened (2 Sam. 13:21) and is, according to the author, "very angry" (ויחר לו מאד). The author is not explicit; we are left to wonder what "all the things" are that anger the king. Tamar's rape? Public exposure and damage to his own reputation?[23] After all, Tamar does not (at first) go quietly into her exile. Whatever has angered the king does not, however, evoke action. It is left to Absalom to balance the books by having Amnon executed, albeit years later, and when he does, David issues no censure of the murder either. And, as we shall see, Absalom arranges Amnon's death for his own ends, not hers. Tamar's fate is only important insofar as it affects *his* grasp on power.

Amnon knows that Absalom is a force to be reckoned with. He is praised more than anyone else in the kingdom for his beauty (2 Sam. 14:25). He is blessed with a head of hair that proclaims his virility.[24] And he is the only son of David's who can claim royal lineage on both sides.[25] When Amnon tells Jonadab his troubles, he specifies clearly whom he is competing with: "I am in love with Tamar, the sister of *my brother Absalom*" (2 Sam. 13:4).[26] Tamar has already been introduced as *Absalom's* sister in 2 Samuel 13:1. Information has been repeated precisely in order to drive the point home. This is a contest between men played out through sexual violence against a woman. Rape is the currency for negotiating status among men.

One prince wants what the other prince has: control over sexual access to Tamar. Gaining that access constitutes a direct attack on Absalom's honor.[27] It would also provide a venue for establishing who has greater authority. Kings (and patriarchs) are supposed to decide who may acquire sexual access to women of the family. A man who has such authority—and Amnon will demonstrate that capacity before a host of men—has won a victory. In raping his half-sister, Amnon tests how far his father's indulgence will permit him to go, while simultaneously issuing a direct challenge to Absalom.

Commentators note that Absalom appears absent of concern for her, though he sees her almost immediately after the assault with her clothes torn, ashes on her head, and crying out in grief and woe (2 Sam. 13:19–20).[28] Absalom seems to know already who has raped her, though his language is disturbingly vague: "Has Amnon your brother been with you?" he asks (13:20). Before she can respond, he commands her to keep quiet. He reminds her that Amnon is her brother and advises her not to take the rape to heart (13:20). Absalom's honor is at stake, not Tamar's humiliation. In a rape culture, men frequently collude to silence "their" women when they have been assaulted by another family member; protecting male honor and reputation is paramount.

Two years after Tamar has been sexually assaulted, Absalom arranges a celebratory gathering. He tries, and fails, to get the king and all his brothers to attend a sheepshearing of his own flocks (2 Sam. 13:23–25). David is reticent and suspicious about whether Amnon, his heir, should go, but Absalom eventually persuades the king that all the princes should take part (13:26–27). In a system governed by hegemonic masculinity, all parties know that battles for dominance are ongoing. The king's concern is to make sure not to lose at that game. Sons struggling for supremacy with one another have no time to challenge him.

The princes are all present; the king is absent. Absalom seizes his opportunity to have Amnon assassinated. The king hears a rumor, however, that Absalom has killed *all* the princes of the realm. He tears his clothing and lies on the floor (2 Sam. 13:30–31). Suddenly, Jonadab becomes, again, a critical player in the narrative, again counseling an apparently incapacitated member of the royal house. Mysteriously, he alone seems to know that the princes are safe. Only Amnon is dead, he tells David, for Absalom decided on this course of action when his sister was violated (13:32). At the chapter's outset, Jonadab seemed to be acting as friend and counselor to the *heir* to the throne. At the close of the chapter, after the rape that he himself enabled, he behaves as if he were *the king's* friend and counselor.

Jonadab, unlike David and the courtiers, expresses no grief—as Amnon's friend, one would expect him to.[29] Instead, it seems he was in on the plan to do away with the heir to the throne. He abets Absalom in making his escape by reminding the court of Tamar's rape and Absalom's right to avenge the insult to his honor. No one who has heard Jonadab's reminder will pursue Absalom for acting as a man should. David, too, is off the hook—he can display his grief over Amnon's death while still permitting Absalom to escape. Perhaps Jonadab "switched sides." Perhaps he was neither Amnon's nor David's friend, but Absalom's.[30]

Ultimately, the rape of Tamar serves Absalom more than any other man of the family. Absalom will be able to remove Amnon, his primary challenger and heir to the throne, proving that he is an ideal man according to biblical hegemonic masculinity's standards—a man who knows how to defend his honor. Absalom will mount an effective rebellion against David, amassing followers and military experts and counselors. Like David, Absalom is beautiful, persuasive, and a successful warrior. And like his father, he will use women and rape women for his own ends.

We have seen the men of the royal family jockey for position and work out their relationships through the conduit of Tamar's body. Sexual violence is the proving ground for their competition. And, as dominant men do both in these texts and in our own time, they can and will enlist the help, support, and even participation of others. Other men—a host of men, in fact—participate, witness, collude in, and enable the rape of Tamar. Who carries the message David sends to Tamar asking her to go to her brother Amnon's rooms (2 Sam. 13:7)? Who accompanies her when she goes? Even if we assume that women were sent to Tamar or that women walked her to her brother's abode, we cannot escape a disturbing reality: Amnon is not alone when she arrives. Neither is he alone when Tamar prepares the pastries (13:8). In fact, Tamar is on display the entire time; made to perform not just for Amnon, but for an assembly of men. Just after she performs her assigned tasks and sets out the food, Amnon issues a command (2 Sam. 13:9). A literal translation might read something like: "Have every man go out, away from me" (הוציאו כל איש מעלי). Amnon orders some of his servants to kick out other men. Some guests are no longer welcome to stay.

But they know what is coming. Tamar has been on exhibit for these men, taking the dough, kneading it, forming it, baking it, presenting it. To make pastry of any kind requires physical exertion and concentrated activity. Fingers must be thrust into dough, which must be slapped, folded, squeezed, and shaped. Pressure must be applied; the upper body leans in and forward, into the work. Who is in this room? One woman, many men. The latter watch Tamar, David's most beautiful daughter, as she works the ingredients, handles them, fashions them into a tasty, mouth-watering product.[31] Everyone knows where the product of her labor is supposed to end. Everyone can guess what will actually happen next. The heart cakes will be left uneaten. It is Tamar who shall be consumed.

Amnon's audience—and the biblical writer's audience too—constitute a crowd of men who are offered a clearly sexualized spectacle. "When men share a social space to collectively enjoy the display of female bodies, they also bond as audience, viewers, and masturbators. When men gather to collectively become aroused, they participate in a male exchange of women" (Flood 2008, 351–52). Amnon is part of the performance. The men who are expelled from the room know why they are being asked to leave. They are being treated, vicariously, to a demonstration of the prince's sexual prowess. As Stone observes: "One's prestige depends in part on one's ability to display in sufficient quantity culturally recognized gender characteristics, including those which concern sexual activity" (1996, 38).

The guests leave. Amnon is now ready to issue his next orders. "Come," he says, "lie with me, my sister" (2 Sam. 13:11). Tamar protests, desperately trying to persuade Amnon not to rape her. To no avail. The prince "would not listen to her; he overpowered her and lay with her by force" (13:14). The biblical author reduces Tamar to a pronoun. The princess is now a nameless "her" (ולא אבה לשמע בקולה ויחזק ממנה ויענה וישכב אתה). After he has raped her, Amnon is filled with hate. The biblical writer pulls no punches, using the word for "hate" (שנא) no less than four times in a single verse (13:15).[32] The person one destroys in pursuit of power becomes a thing. "It" is disgusting because "it" has been destroyed, whether "it" is a human corpse on a battlefield, the broken remains of a death camp prisoner, or the body of a raped woman. And so, after the rape, Amnon orders Tamar to "get out!" (2 Sam. 13:15). "She pleaded with him, 'Please don't commit this wrong; to send me away would be even worse than the first wrong you committed against me.' But he would not listen to her" (13:16).[33] Amnon is uninterested in Tamar's fate. She has served as a vehicle for challenging Absalom and is now mere refuse that must be disposed of. What happens to Tamar is only important insofar as it furthers a story of men competing for sovereignty and supremacy.

Amnon calls an attendant to rid him of his victim (2 Sam. 13:17). Though translations routinely "fix" the text, adding the word "woman" to Amnon's command, there is no "woman" in the Hebrew text. The Hebrew does not read "Get *that woman* out of my presence" but "Get *this* out of my presence" (שלחו נא את־זאת מעלי החוצה). Amnon is polite to the man he commands, using the particle *na* (נא), to indicate entreaty. Tamar is, however, reduced to a disposable object. If we wanted to make clear how polite Amnon is to the servant and how brutal he is to Tamar, we might translate this verse so: "Please, get *this* out of my presence, outside." The servant does as he is ordered: he throws Tamar out and bars the door (13:18).[34]

It is not clear whether Amnon is wholly alone with Tamar during the rape. Amnon's servant, if not already present, is clearly close at hand. Moreover, the form of Amnon's command to the servant is in the plural imperative form (שלחו). We know that a number of men *were* in the room prior to the rape. Amnon directs servants to escort his guests out, using a plural form (2 Sam. 13:9). Now he decrees, again in the plural, that Tamar be thrown out.

"His servant" (נערו) is, conversely, in the singular. Is the audience offered a subtext which implies that Amnon's men are close at hand, within earshot, listening to what transpires? Is the audience meant to wonder whether all of Amnon's servants left the room with the guests they were charged to expel? Is the biblical writer inviting his audience to populate their imagination with men present during the prelude, the act, and the aftermath of Tamar's rape?

Certainly, a host of men know what has happened to Tamar. Men look on as she labors. Some likely hear or witness, as bystanders, the rape. At least one additional man throws Tamar out of Amnon's rooms; others could have heard her lament. Two years later, Jonadab will publicly remind David's courtiers and servants of the rape (2 Sam. 13:32). By this time, a wide circle of men has witnessed, colluded, and heard about what has happened to Tamar, including family members, courtiers, and servants. David's entire court is complicit.

Voyeurism is an essential part of this narrative.[35] Biblical authors write scenes of men engaged in sex talk, in fantasy, in indecent exposure of themselves and their women, and in sexual violence. They picture men picturing what other men do to women. They describe men listening and watching too. These texts were composed by men for men; inviting voyeurism is a way to reinforce biblical hegemonic masculinity and to cement its rape culture. Even modern readers—and of any gender identity—are cast into the role of voyeur by these texts.[36] And we are likewise implicated if we do not call out exactly what is happening: sexual violence is being used as a medium for negotiating male status and male bonds. Tamar's rape is about what the men of the Hebrew Bible can do with it, not about what they do to her.

2 Samuel 16: The Rape of the *Pilagshim*

By the time we read of the rape of David's *pilagshim*, Absalom has long since done away with Amnon and launched an open rebellion against his father. To that end he has engaged in important displays of influence and prowess. He acquires a chariot and arranges for a cadre of fifty men to run before him (2 Sam. 15:1). It is audacious, really, the sort of pomp and circumstance that broadcasts his claim to royal rank, as Robert Alter rightly notes (1999, 283 n. 1). The prince brazenly takes up a position at the gates of Jerusalem to solicit every Israelite he can. He addresses each man who enters the city. David, he insists, would not even deign to hear their complaints. Were *he*, Absalom, to be made judge (שפט) in his father's stead, however, he could not only guarantee a hearing, but also the best of all possible outcomes. Those who apply to him for aid will receive both justice *and* favor (15:4).[37] As Seth Sanders notes, Absalom cleverly suggests he be made a "judge" in place of his father (2019, 522). The prince is appealing to older ideas about how Israel should be governed, ideas that valorize the man who *earns* honor, respect, and the right to reign as a righteous judge.[38]

Ideal male behaviors are made evident through narrative repetition. When David finally agrees to see Absalom long after his execution of Amnon, Absalom shows honor to the king by prostrating before him. David kisses his son, signaling that Absalom's presence is accepted at the royal court once again (2 Sam. 14:33). David's kiss is clearly a political act, not a paternal one. He is proving who wields authority. The Hebrew text hammers the point home: it is "the king," not just "David," who makes the gesture. Kissing Absalom signals David's superiority and his sovereignty; a king shows whom he accepts as a subordinate through ritualized acts of intimacy.

Absalom, however, wants honor and rank for himself. He performs the same ritual act his father used before him in order to enact *his* superiority over other men. Standing at the gates of the city that his father ostensibly rules, Absalom waits for the men of Israel to come before him to declare their fealty. Each time a man approaches and prepares to prove his allegiance by bowing before the prince (להשתחות לו), Absalom extends his hand. And then, the text tells us, Absalom "took hold" (והחזיק לו) of his new recruit and sealed the deal with a kiss (2 Sam. 15:5). The man who shows himself ready to bend down before the man who would be king makes his subordinate position obvious and offers honor to his superior. It is Absalom who performs control here, not David.

The prince brings men to him with speech; he binds them through the body. Is this, perhaps, a homoerotic moment? Sexual overtones are present in the text, overtones that suggest that Absalom not only resembles his father, but his brother, too. Amnon "took hold" (ויחזק ממנה) of Tamar before he raped her. Absalom takes hold (והחזיק לו) of Israelite men before kissing them. As David Halperin notes, "within the horizons of the male world . . . hierarchy itself is hot" (2000, 99).

Both princes clutch at what they want. In both cases, what they want is power. The men of the royal family are all contenders for dominion because they are all engaging in the well-worn tactics that biblical hegemonic masculinity valorizes—audacious shows of strength, persuasive and manipulative speech, and the use of sex and sexual violence in the pursuit of clout and, even, the throne. Absalom does not mask his challenges to his father's rule, but this too is characteristic of the biblical hegemonic system. Men who want supremacy, like men who have it, must engage in fearless displays of potency—whether martial or sexual. Such displays are exciting, and they are meant to be witnessed and acknowledged by other men. Their tacit or explicit approval translates into honor, status, and authority.

Despite his son's obvious and public posturing, David makes no attempt to thwart Absalom, just as he made no attempt to thwart Amnon. In fact, David grants both sons his permission to take potentially threatening actions. Amnon presented his own aims in sexual terms; nevertheless, David was enlisted in the project and himself summoned Tamar to her brother's rooms. Absalom, in turn, openly asked his father for permission to go discharge an unspecified vow at Hebron, the city where David himself was crowned; Absalom went, however, not to fulfill a vow, but to be crowned in David's stead. Hints and allusions to potential and dangerous moves that would wrest both legitimacy and authority out of the king's hands are rife here, just as they were with Amnon. Is David ignoring Absalom's power grab or propitiating his son? A messenger arrives and openly announces what the king must surely already suspect: "The loyalty of the men of Israel has veered toward Absalom" (2 Sam. 15:13). David, in turn, insists that the court must flee. It appears that Absalom has won a critical victory; he is the ideal man and King David is, it would seem, ceding the field of battle.

All his household (וכל ביתו) went with him, all but ten *pilagshim* (2 Sam. 15:16). These, David leaves behind to "mind" the palace (ויעזב המלך את עשר נשים פלגשים לשמר הבית). This curious announcement is followed by information that only makes it more puzzling, for the biblical author is at pains to enumerate and describe all those David *does* take with him, emphasizing the totality of David's followers by repeatedly using the word "all" (כל). It is quite the crowd. The king is followed by "*all* the people" (כל העם), *all* his servants and followers (כל עבדיו), *all* the Cherethites, the Pelethites, and the Gittites, (15:17–18). Children, too, are part of the king's entourage (15:22).

Scholars have tried to explain why David would hurry out of Jerusalem with courtiers, men at arms, and servants, only to leave his *pilagshim* to "keep" or "guard" (לשמר) his palace. Alter regards David's decision as either a desperate gesture of hope that he will return to reclaim his wives, or as an act of fatalism—comparing it to the way David tells Ittai the Gittite, his faithful follower, to return to Jerusalem once Absalom takes over the city and "stay with the king" (2 Sam. 15:20). But this seems unlikely; David plays the same game here with Ittai as he has done earlier with Jonathan, using dramatic speech to invoke protestations of unconditional loyalty.[39] Andrew Hill argues that David acquired the women as a purely political move in the process of securing alliances with the Jebusites who had formerly administered Jerusalem. He suggests that the *pilagshim* were royal Jebusite citizens who must remain in the Jebusite stronghold. David has no choice but to leave them there (2006, 135–36). Karen Engelken believes David left his harem behind in order to test Absalom's ambitions (1990, 78–79). Since the prince has already had himself crowned in Hebron, it is hard to know what more David could test.

Source critics have noted that the word *pilagshim* comes after *nashim*, the word for "wives" (נשים פלגשים) in 2 Samuel 15:16. In the whole of the Hebrew Bible, these terms are otherwise reversed—only in this narrative do the *pilagshim* get named, seemingly, as wives, as *nashim*. These scholars explain the episode as an editorial addition inserted in order to ensure that the narrative fulfills Yhwh's announcement that he himself will give David's women to another man (2 Sam. 12:11–12). They argue that 2 Samuel 15:16 was a later addition because a later editor bungled the word order. The verse stands out because it was patched into the earlier narrative (Langlamet 1976, 352; Engelken 1990, 78). But a standard phrase, one well-known enough to be deployed repeatedly, is unlikely to pose challenges to later authors. Moreover, Yhwh also deploys the term *nashim* in his threat. It is just as possible to argue that a deliberate editorial decision was made here, one that would serve to emphasize the insult to David's honor and virility. We are meant to focus on that first word. We are meant to understand that it is David's *wives* whom Absalom rapes.

David leaves his *pilagshim* entirely to the mercy of Absalom and his men, just as he leaves Tamar to Amnon. This may well be a propitiating move, a way to offer his son(s) an illusion of control. In the struggle for the throne, the king's behavior suggests that he has lost the first rounds with both his heir and the prince who plans to supplant him. But who is the man who wins in the end? David remains king. Both sons die. Yhwh sticks to his promises: David is beloved of Yhwh, and nothing will change Yhwh's commitment to him; his throne is eternal. "Your house and your kingship shall ever be secure before you; your throne shall be established forever," Yhwh has promised him (2 Sam. 7:16).[40]

Ken Stone has argued that the episode of the *pilagshim* is a way to declare not merely that David is no longer king, but that he is no longer a man. In effect, the text makes it obvious that David is unable to manage sexual access to his women:

> Absalom's sexual activity with his father's concubines can be read as an attempt to attack David's gender-based prestige, rather than as a simple declaration that David is no longer king. By having sexual relations with the ten concubines of David, Absalom has demonstrated David's inability to fulfill a crucial part of a culturally inscribed view of masculinity. As all Israel can see, David has been unable to maintain control over sexual access to the women of his house, and so has failed with regard to what is, in many cultures, a critical criterion for the assessment of manhood.
>
> (1996, 121)[41]

By raping David's *pilagshim*, Stone argues, Absalom has proven himself the better man.[42] Absalom has appropriately avenged his sister to protect his honor (124–25). He has simultaneously made it clear that David is now bereft of honor. The king is "symbolically emasculated" (122) just as he was when his messengers to the Ammonites had their buttocks exposed and their beards half shaven (2 Sam. 10:4). David makes sure that he will not be embarrassed publicly by his messengers. If they show up at court, they become a visible reminder of the honor he has lost. He orders them to stay at Jericho until their beards have grown back. Only then are they permitted to return (2 Sam. 10:5). But if David were good at being a man, he would ensure his messengers never experience shaming and he would never hand his women over to another man (1996, 123).

There is a catch, here—Absalom is not the man to suggest the rape of the *pilagshim*; David's former counselor, Ahithophel, does. Both of David's sons are advised to rape. Like Amnon, Absalom is following the suggestion of his most important advisor. If he shows himself to be the better man by raping David's *pilagshim*, it is only because he is taking advice from another important man. The rapist is not acting alone. Men support each other in planning and committing sexual violence, both in the Hebrew Bible as in our own time.

Men ally for power. Sexual violence is a tool when they clash. The rape of Tamar may have begun as Amnon's effort to challenge Absalom, but it eventually serves as an opportunity for Absalom to assert his command over the prince and heir and to have his competition killed off. The rape of the *pilagshim* is a way for Absalom to assert his dominance over David. Absalom, like his brother before him, will lose his bid for authority and he, too, will be murdered by another male member of the family. In struggles for rule, sexual violence against women can be an intermediary step toward the murder of men.

In a rape culture, sexual assault is the outcome of collaboration among men. Tamar's rape was planned by Jonadab, once counselor to Amnon. Absalom's rape of his father's *pilagshim* is planned by Ahithophel, once counselor to David. Jonadab may have switched sides in a contest between princes; Ahithophel clearly switches sides in the contest between king and prince. Both men counsel sexual violence; both orchestrate rape. Men of David's house and inner circle become turncoats. Brother against brother. Son against father. Friend against friend. Advisor against advisee. Men change sides in struggles for rank and sovereignty.

Absalom sends for Ahithophel early, after heading for Hebron to be crowned in his father's stead, and the wise elder counselor appears eager to help. The conspiracy is gaining strength, we are told; the men of Israel are going Absalom's way (2 Sam. 15:12). And while David works to plant spies in Absalom's midst, Absalom has already been winning over David's former advisors.

Why does Ahithophel abandon David? As David is fleeing Jerusalem, Shimei, a man from Saul's clan, hurls rocks and insults at the king. Yhwh is paying the king back, Shimei proclaims, for what he did to his master's house. Yhwh is handing the kingdom to Absalom because of the king's own evil (2 Sam. 16:8). David, he adds, is a man of blood (והנך ברעתך כי איש דמים אתה).

The blood on David's hands is Uriah's, of course. That blood may be of personal interest to Ahithophel. An Ahithophel, a Gilonite, father to Eliam, appears in 2 Samuel 23:34. Eliam is Bathsheba's father (2 Sam. 11:3) and a member of David's thirty mighty men (2 Sam. 23:8–39).[43] If Eliam's father of 2 Samuel 23 is the same Ahithophel we meet in 2 Samuel 15:12, then Ahithophel is, perchance, grandfather of David's wife, Bathsheba, and thus closely connected to David's inner circle. Kinship is political, and its networks, then and now, are important.

David himself, upon hearing that Ahithophel has joined Absalom, prays directly to the deity for help. He should. The biblical author tells us that Ahithophel's counsel "was accepted like an oracle sought from God" (2 Sam. 16:23) and not only by Absalom, but by David before him. "Please, O LORD," David implores, "frustrate Ahithophel's counsel!" (2 Sam. 15:31). Yhwh seems to answer the king post haste by sending him his loyal servant Hushai in the very next verse (2 Sam. 15:32). David takes advantage of what (or who) appears heaven-sent; he arranges for Hushai to join Absalom's camp to act as his spy. And it will be Hushai who frustrates Ahithophel's counsel, supporting his king and friend.

We should make note, however, that Hushai will have no objection to Ahithophel's advice that the prince rape his father's women before all Israel and in the full light of day.[44] Like all the other men around Absalom, Hushai becomes a participant, enabler, and colluder in sexual violence. It will all happen, indeed, where it can be vicariously experienced and even seen by those men: directly on the roof from which David once ogled Ahithophel's granddaughter. David took Bathsheba from her husband; Ahithophel makes sure that Absalom takes the *pilagshim* from David. Ahithophel regains some of his own honor, as one of the men responsible for sexual access to the women of his family, and, at the same time, he offers Absalom a way to show just what kind of man (and king) he can be. An ideal man in the Hebrew Bible is one who acquires, takes, and rapes women.[45]

Ahithophel has pragmatic considerations too: he knows that once Absalom rapes the *pilagshim*, all of Israel will know that there can be no reconciliation between father and son. The Hebrew root deployed here (באש) literally means "stink." "All Israel," Ahithophel is suggesting, "will know that you stink to your father" (2 Sam. 16:21).[46] Once all Israel knows that there can be no turning back, they will fight, by necessity, all the harder for their newly crowned king. Ahithophel is doing his best to ensure that his side, the side he has thrown his lot in with, will win not just the battle for Jerusalem, but the war for the kingdom.

Ahithophel gives advice while Hushai is present. Absalom makes note of that fact. When he asks Ahithophel for guidance, he uses both second- and first-person plural forms. He asks Ahithophel directly and Hushai indirectly what "we" should do (2 Sam. 16:20). Perhaps the prince is testing Hushai. Hushai, when he arrives, calls out "long live the king! Long live the king!" (2 Sam. 16:16). Absalom is skeptical. "Is this your loyalty to your friend?" he asks. "Why didn't you go with your friend?" (16:17). The use of the term "friend" is indicative—it is both a court title and as a sign of intimacy. Absalom must make sure: will Hushai protest Ahithophel's council to rape his father's women? Doing so constitutes an unforgiveable assault on David's honor, after all.

Jonathan Grossman suggests that Hushai approves the rape of the *pilagshim* because he knows that the rape is Yhwh's will (2007, 562). Ahithophel is working on behalf of the deity; Absalom is Yhwh's proxy.[47] This deity oversees, legislates, and even models the behaviors that support a rape culture. In such a culture, sexual violence is a means for negotiating power. The best way for one man to humiliate another and challenge his supremacy is to take and rape his women.

Hushai wants to support David. Ahithophel's counsel that Absalom rape his father's *pilagshim* is not, in the end, the advice Hushai must hinder. In a world in which male clashes for dominance override all else, it is important to save David; it is immaterial what happens to his women. They are no more than collateral damage. The plan that might give Absalom the kingdom is the stratagem Hushai must thwart. And so Hushai first solicits Absalom's trust, becoming part of an intimate circle of men who actively collude in the prince's sexual assault. Then, as David's spy, Hushai can do maximum damage to Absalom's cause by putting a stop to Ahithophel when it matters most. After the rape, Hushai argues against Ahithophel's counsel to attack David immediately (2 Sam. 17:1), suggesting instead that Absalom wait, gather his forces, and face his father in the field (2 Sam. 17:11). Absalom takes Hushai's bad advice. It will lead to his death.

Absalom may do the raping, but all of his counselors are fully in support. They even pitch a tent for him on the roof of the palace, the text tells us (2 Sam. 16:22), and Absalom violates the women "before the eyes of all Israel" (לעיני כל ישראל). Who is "all Israel"? Absalom's advisors, his generals, his soldiers, his servants, his courtiers. Once again, a mass of men is complicit in rape. Absalom exhibits his virility by raping no fewer than ten women before his men. His men see what kind of stuff it takes to become king: sexual predation on a grand scale.

Once again voyeurism is essential. The sex is heard, even watched. Again, the male biblical audience is given a scene to imagine, pornographic action they can visualize vicariously. And once again, the modern reader who does not name this narrative for what it is—a story of licensed violation of women, witnessed by a crowd of men—becomes an accomplice, a bystander, or even, potentially, a colluder.

In the end, Absalom will die a terrible death, just as his brother did. Neither dies as punishment for being a rapist. They die because they have lost battles for status and rank. The rapes of Tamar and the *pilagshim* demonstrate the battles they won. Their deaths demonstrate that they lost the war. Amnon is made drunk, too drunk to defend himself, before he is executed. He becomes the fool before Israel because he is so easily outmaneuvered by Absalom; he pays no penalty, as Tamar argued he would, for raping her (2 Sam. 13:13). His death, however, takes place in a setting replete with sexual associations—pastoral festivals are locations for sex and licentiousness in ancient Israel, where men get drunk, and where celebration is a setting for both deceit and for death.[48] His execution makes it clear that Absalom is better than Amnon at acting the man, and Absalom's performance includes his superior sexual power and sexual violence.

Absalom, in turn, dies at the hands of Joab in a scene that is again, replete with sexual allusions. Caught in a terebinth by his luscious hair, the hair that signaled his virility, he is helpless to defend himself. He dies being repeatedly penetrated. Joab is the first to pierce the prince, taking three sharp darts and driving them into Absalom's heart (2 Sam. 18:14). Ten of his armor-bearers join in the execution, striking Absalom until he dies. Perhaps the number of men is meant to remind us of the number of women Absalom raped. Sexual violence is an interim step in negotiating power; murder and execution of the enemy is the final one.[49]

Conclusions

In the Hebrew Bible, men who command engage in ongoing contests for rank and rule. Sexual violence serves as an instrument for negotiating power. Neither the rape of Tamar nor the rape of the *pilagshim* is about the women involved, but rather about the way the men of David's house establish their right to authority and control. And when men in the royal family challenge each other's might, they do not compete alone. A host of men engages in such competitions; a multitude of men participate, collude, and enable the rapists.

All the men of Israel become, in the end, bystanders, participants, witnesses, and agents of the rape of women. Dominant men rape women, and they give women to other men to be raped. By offering their subordinates such opportunities, men who lead keep them loyal. Men bond through sexual violence in the narratives of the Hebrew Bible, just as they do in our time. These narratives feature, on occasion, subordinate men who do refuse to carry out orders of their superiors,[50] but not when it comes to the rape of women. Messengers and councilors, courtiers and servants, soldiers and generals—they are all part and parcel of the rape culture biblical literature describes and even valorizes. Rape in the house of David is made permissible by a company of men.

Notes

1 Clines includes being musical as a feature of idealized masculinity; this claim has been disputed. Stephen Wilson suggests that self-control is valued (2015, 39–40).
2 Esther Fuchs has noted "the threat posed to the patriarchal order" (2003, 217, 223). I disagree, however, with her reading that 2 Samuel 13 "is unambiguous in its indictment of the rapist and vindication of the avenger" (202).
3 See Introduction, note 12.
4 Women have "a kind of ultimate importance in the schema of men's gender constitution—representing an absolute of exchange value, of representation itself" (Sedgwick 1985, 134).
5 Sexual activity in the Hebrew Bible is important, as Ken Stone writes, because of the consequences for male relationships (1996, 136). Victor Matthews and Don Benjamin argue that rape in ancient Israel was not only an act of violence, but a social institution used by one household of men to test the honor of another (1997, 339). William Propp writes: "From the biblical perspective, rape is an affair between men" (1993, 41).
6 Scholars have noted that the most effective forums for male bonding include sex either witnessed or shared by other men. Men become friends as an outcome of shared sexual experience. See Prohaska and Gailey 2010, *passim*; Yancey Martin and Hummer 1989, *passim*; Bird 1996, *passim*; Boswell and Spade 1996, *passim*. Flood explores how shared heterosexual sex facilitates homosocial bonding, regardless of whether it manifests as a jointly imagined fantasy, a show put on for the men, or the performance of sex acts. One subject describes arranging for his friend and for himself to have sex with their girlfriends within earshot of one another and describes the experience as "teamwork" of the best kind. Another subject, asked whom he considered a good friend, answered: "the other guy on the other end of a pig on a spit" (2008, 350).
7 As I argue in *Male Friendship, Homosociality, and Women in the Hebrew Bible*, 2022, *passim*.
8 Amnon, son of Ahinoam of Jezreel, is introduced in 2 Samuel 3:2; and Absalom, David's third son by Maacah (daughter of King Talmai of Geshur), in 2 Samuel 3:3. Scholars have long noted that 2 Samuel 11 is replete with familial references, e.g., Phyllis Trible 1984, 38.

9 Stone states that incest is not the issue. That Tamar is a virgin is what makes it impossible for Amnon to "do anything to her" (1996, 107). Fokkelien Van Dijk-Hemmes agrees (1989, 139).
10 Throughout this work, I have chosen to use the translation of the Jewish Study Bible, in large part because it is easily accessible together with the Hebrew text at www.sefaria.org/texts. Here, however, I choose to translate more literally than the Jewish Study Bible, which renders the Hebrew as "Was it your brother Amnon who did this to you?"
11 Gayle Rubin writes: "Kinship systems do not merely exchange women. They exchange sexual access, genealogical statuses, lineage names and ancestors, rights and people—men, women, and children—in concrete systems of social relationships" (1997, 38).
12 See also Alter 1999, 265 n. 3. Olyan does not agree, arguing that 13:3 "implies that Amnon has other 'friends'" (2017, 157–58 n. 97).
13 Van Dijk-Hemmes argues that Jonadab is aware that only David can remove obstacles for Amnon regarding Tamar (1989, 140). Amy Kalmanofsky makes a similar claim (2014, 104).
14 The son born as a result of David's rape of Bathsheba dies in infancy—the first casualty (literally speaking) of a fourfold indemnity he himself decreed. See Frymer-Kensky 2002, 154–56.
15 This wordplay is also found in Genesis 39:6. We learn that Potiphar had left all he had in his trusted servant Joseph's hands because he had no concern about anything "save the food he ate" (אם הלחם אשר הוא אוכל). Rabbinic commentators claim that when Joseph insists that he has control over everything but *lechem*, he is referring to the woman Potiphar regularly consumed, his wife. For this reason, the rabbis align Genesis 39:6 with Proverbs 30:20, where eating (presumably *lechem*) clearly refers to sex. "Such is the way of an adulteress: She eats, wipes her mouth, and says: 'I have done no wrong' " (כן דרך אשה מנאפת אכלה ומחתה פיה ואמרה לא פעלתי און).
16 The term is used in Genesis 41:2, 5, 7, 18, and 20 to make a clear contrast between sickly, ugly cows and healthy (or fat), beautiful ones, as well as between healthy ears of grain and scorched and blighted ones.
17 Van Dijk-Hemmes also suggests such a possibility (1989, 140), as does Kalmanofsky (2014, 106).
18 Ryan Higgins notes that David's use of the particle *na* (נא), which indicates polite entreaty, is a way to make his command both "innocent and polite" and to defray suspicion (2020, 39).
19 Prohaska and Gailey describe a "hogging" contest in which men lure heavy women to have sex. Afterwards, the men discuss what happened. Sometimes they hide in the room. The shock the woman experiences when the men leap out of hiding to witness and take part in her degradation is part of the attraction (2010, 19–20).
20 David announces his own outrage at those who have done away with his enemies, and maintains his own innocence. See 2 Samuel 1:14–15, 2 Samuel 3:28, and 2 Samuel 4:11.
21 See 1 Samuel 24:4–8 and 1 Samuel 26:11–25.
22 Jonathan will act against King Saul, his own father, on David's behalf.
23 Some believe David to be shocked and surprised. See, for example, Dietrich 2007, 120. Kurtis Peters argues that David could not have known what was going to happen, or else he would have no reason to be angry when he heard "all

the things" (2021, 316). Danna Fewell and David Gunn note suggest he is angry because he feels caught out (1993, 145).

24 A profusion of body hair signifies virility (Stone 1996, 122). Absalom's hair is described just before his children are named, connecting the appearance and the performance of virility (124).

25 Absalom's mother, after all, is the queen of Geshur. Kalmanofsky concludes that Amnon is unconcerned with breaking an incest prohibition. He knows that Absalom would never relinquish Tamar. Absalom would fear that if Tamar and Amnon were married, they would both be preserving the purity of David's line and securing Amnon's position as heir (2014, 104).

26 The Hebrew root for "love" (אהב) does not simply denote affection. In the Hebrew Bible, just as in modern English, one can "love" a kind of food (Gen. 27:9) or an object that one wants to consume.

27 Matthews and Benjamin suggest that Amnon's rape of Tamar is about honor, control, and territory and constitutes a hostile takeover against Absalom's household. Kinship is political, as is rape (1997, 350).

28 There are scholars who conclude otherwise. See, for example, Trible, who believes Absalom to be an "advocate" for Tamar (1984, 51) and Dominic Rudman, who describes Absalom addressing his sister "tenderly" (1998, 330).

29 Jonadab's absence of grief is telling (Olyan 2017, 31, 36).

30 Olyan wonders if Jonadab became Absalom's confidant after the rape (2017, 82). I suggest that it could have been planned at the start by Absalom and Jonadab, "whose secret friendship we must uncover, step by awful step" (2022, 78).

31 "Practices of preparing and eating food," Elspeth Probyn points out, "are highly sensual and sometimes sexual. . . . The more mundane stuffing of a chicken may bypass the question of its sex, but nonetheless intimately involves the cook thrusting her hands, covered in buttery crumbs, up the open orifice (you wouldn't use a spoon, would you?)" (2000, 59).

32 We could translate: "Then Amnon *hated* her, a great *hatred* indeed; the *hatred* with which he *hated* her was greater than the lust he had felt for her." The root deployed here, *sanah* (שׂנא), also appears in Deuteronomy 22:13 and 24:3 to describe the feelings a husband would have for a woman he despised enough to want to divorce. Having sex with a woman effectively connotes marriage (Stone 2015, 175)—hating her connotes divorce.

33 When a rapist of a virgin is discovered, biblical law commands him to marry his victim (Deut. 22:28–29). Stone writes: "We may have here the projection of an 'official' position via the voice of a female character" (1996, 115).

34 Amnon's servants are party to Tamar's rape. Whether it is anticipated, overheard, or witnessed, sexual violence is, on some level, mutually experienced by the male characters of the text. Modern studies suggest that "a homosocially focused social life is associated with attitudes conducive to the sexual harassment of women." Increases in behavioral aggression against women follow exposure to pornography, particularly if the pornography is violent in nature (Flood and Pease 2009, 134–35).

35 In Genesis 26:8, Isaac "plays" with his wife in full view of King Abimelech and, potentially, of other men (Thiede 2022, 100–1). Harold Washington suggests that Tamar's "memory as a delectable rape victim . . . is preserved in her niece and namesake, Absalom's daughter Tamar, 'a beautiful woman'" (353). Although Alter argues that Tamar's niece cannot have been born after the rape

42 Disposing of Daughters, Sisters, and Wives

of her aunt (1999, 281 n. 27), readers are likely experiencing associations rather than parsing generations.

36 Clines presents the Song of Songs as a voyeuristic fantasy written by men for men and notes that the Song was performed by men for men, too (2009, 94–121). The Bible attests to such performances (Ezek. 33:31–32).

37 J.P. Fokkelman notes iterative forms in the text; we are reading one example of what Absalom has done and said, "with minor variations hundreds of times" (1981, 166). Absalom is a clever and ambitious politician who gains followers by showing interest in their fate.

38 Sanders notes that the term deployed here has both juridical and political connotations (2019, 520). The deity, too, possesses his place because he is the true judge of all he has created (Gen. 18:25). Absalom is a chip off the old block. In his own youth, David, too, was capable of brazen acts of self-promotion, including publicly (and repeatedly) asking Saul's troops about the reward they claim the king has offered for killing Goliath. By repeatedly asking about a presumed royal prize, by going from one set of men to another, David ensures that Saul will have to give him one (1 Sam. 17:26–27, 30). Then as now, those who are politically savvy know that frequent repetition of a claim takes on the appearance of affirming a reality.

39 It is a typical move for David. When David insists Jonathan execute him himself rather than bring him back to Saul (1 Sam. 20:8), Jonathan invokes his own death at Yhwh's hands if he prove unfaithful to his friend (20:13). Jonathan explicitly disavows any claim he has, as Saul's eldest son, to the throne. Ittai, too, will be compelled by David's apparent abdication of the throne to offer his utter devotion and will likewise invoke Yhwh as witness (2 Sam. 15:21).

40 David Tombs (2017) makes a similar suggestion, asking: "Was David willing to explore some form of pact or power-share with his son, and therefore attempted to 'sweeten the deal' by gifting him 'his' women? Perhaps he saw these women as an acceptable price to buy Absalom off, or to soften his anger, or even to distract him temporarily from pursuing his father."

41 David's lack of virility is a subject in his waning years, when the virgin Abishag is brought to his bed to warm him. Despite her beauty and youth, the king did not (could not?) "know her" (1 Kings 1:4).

42 Stone avoids the word *rape*, instead referring to Absalom's "sexual activity" or "sexual relations." While male biblical writers will not term what they depict as a rape culture, we should.

43 Uriah the Hittite, Bathsheba's husband, is another.

44 As Yhwh foretold through the prophet Nathan (2 Sam. 12:11–12).

45 Scholars have seen Ahithophel as a crafty man cleverly enacting his revenge for what David did to Bathsheba. Frymer-Kensky writes that "[t]o a wise man, revenge is a dish best tasted cold" (2002, 156). Jon Levenson and Baruch Halpern describe the narrator as "sufficiently subtle (or guileless) to have Bathsheba's grandfather instigate the exaction of YHWH's pound of flesh" (1980, 514).

46 Jacob condemns Reuben for defiling his bed by sleeping with his *pilegesh*, Bilhah (Gen. 49:4).

47 Grossman notes that the *ketiv* version of the text suggests that Ahithophel got his advice *directly* from Yhwh (2007, 561–62).

48 Pastoral festivals at the end of harvest seasons are associated in the ancient Near East with the fertility they celebrate. Such festivities of ancient Israel may have featured *hieros gamos* (sacred marriage) rituals, marking a "licentious, bucolic

occasion" (Wright 1981, 56). Such occasions featured "ritual fornication with the magic intention of securing rich crops and increase of herds" (Astour 1966, 193). At other festivals, Jacob sneaks away from Laban (Gen. 31); Abigail's foolish drunkard of a husband dies, leaving her free to marry David (1 Sam. 25); and Judah has sex with his daughter-in-law, Tamar (Gen. 38).

49 For those who lose contests, not for those who win them. The Levite not only passes his *pilegesh* to the men who will gang rape her, he butchers her thereafter (it is not explicitly said that she is dead at that point). He wins his contest, mustering Yhwh's support in a holy war against those who have insulted him, and, thus, the deity he represents. See Thiede 2022, 110–33.

50 Joab attacks the messenger who tells him that Absalom is helplessly hanging in a terebinth for not killing the prince immediately. The servant reminds the general that David had ordered Joab, Abishai, and Ittai to treat Absalom gently (2 Sam. 18:12–13).

Bibliography

Alter, Robert. *The David Story: A Translation with Commentary of 1 and 2 Samuel*. New York: Norton, 1999.

Astour, Michael C. "Tamar the Hierodule: An Essay in the Method of Vestigial Motifs." *Journal of Biblical Literature* 85, no. 2 (June 1966): 185–96.

Bakon, Shimon. "Jonadab, 'Friend' of Amnon." *Jewish Bible Quarterly* 43, no. 2 (2015): 101–5.

Bird, Sharon R. "Welcome to the Men's Club: Homosociality and the Maintenance of Hegemonic Masculinity." *Gender & Society* 10, no. 2 (April 1996): 120–32. doi:10.1177/089124396010002002.

Boswell, A. Ayers, and Joan Z. Spade. "Fraternities and Collegiate Rape Culture: Why Are Some Fraternities More Dangerous Places for Women?" *Gender & Society* 10, no. 2 (April 1996): 133–47. doi:10.1177/089124396010002003.

Clines, David J.A. *Interested Parties: The Ideology of Writers and Readers of the Hebrew Bible*. Sheffield: Sheffield Phoenix Press, 2009.

Connell, R.W. *Masculinities*, 2nd ed. Berkeley and Los Angeles: University of California Press, 2005.

Dietrich, Walter. "David, Amnon und Abschalom (2 Samuel 13): Literarische, textliche und historische Erwägungen zu den ambivalenten Beziehungen eines Vaters zu seinen Söhnen." *Textus* 23 (2007): 115–43.

Engelken, Karen. *Frauen im Alten Israel: Eine begriffsgeschichtliche und sozialrechtliche Studie zur Stellung der Frau im Alten Testament*. Stuttgart: Kohlhammer, 1990.

Fewell, Danna Nolan, and David M. Gunn. *Gender, Power, and Promise: The Subject of the Bible's First Story*. Nashville: Abingdon Press, 1993.

Flood, Michael. "Men, Sex, and Homosociality: How Bonds Between Men Shape Their Sexual Relations with Women." *Men and Masculinities* 10, no. 3 (2008): 339–59. doi:10.1177/1097184X06287761.

Flood, Michael, and Bob Pease. "Factors Influencing Attitudes to Violence Against Women." *Trauma, Violence, & Abuse* 10, no. 2 (2009): 125–42.

Fokkelman, J.P. *Narrative Art and Poetry in the Books of Samuel: A Full Interpretation Based on Stylistic and Structural Analyses, vol. 1 King David*. Assen, The Netherlands: Van Gorcum, 1981.

Frymer-Kensky, Tikva. *Reading the Women of the Bible: A New Interpretation of Their Stories*. New York: Schocken Books, 2002.

Fuchs, Esther. *Sexual Politics in the Biblical Narrative: Reading the Hebrew Bible as a Woman*. Sheffield: Sheffield Academic Press, 2003.

Grossman, Jonathan. "The Design of the 'Dual Causality' Principle in the Narrative of Absalom's Rebellion." *Biblica* 88, no. 4 (2007): 558–66.

Halperin, David M. "How to Do the History of Male Homosexuality." *GLQ: A Journal of Lesbian and Gay Studies* 6, no. 1 (2000): 87–123. doi:10.1215/10642684-6-1-87.

Higgins, Ryan S. "He Would Not Hear Her Voice: From Skilled Speech to Silence in 2 Samuel 13:1–22." *Journal of Feminist Studies in Religion* 36, no. 2 (2020): 25–42.

Hill, Andrew E. "On David's 'Taking' and 'Leaving' Concubines (2 Samuel 5:13; 15:16)." *Journal of Biblical Literature* 125, no. 1 (2006): 129–39. doi:10.2307/27638350.

Kalmanofsky, Amy. *Dangerous Sisters of the Hebrew Bible*. Minneapolis: Fortress Press, 2014.

Langlamet, F. "Pour ou Contre Salomon?: La Rédaction Prosalomonienne de 1 Rois, I-II." *Revue Biblique* 83, no. 3 (July 1976): 321–79.

Levenson, Jon Douglas, and Baruch Halpern. "The Political Import of David's Marriages." *Journal of Biblical Literature* 99, no. 4 (1980): 507–18.

Matthews, Victor H., and Don C. Benjamin. "Amnon and Tamar: A Matter of Honor (2 Samuel 13:1–38)." In *Crossing Boundaries and Linking Horizons: Studies in Honor of Michael C. Astour on His 80th Birthday*, edited by Gordon Douglas Young, Mark William Chavalas, Richard E. Averbeck, and Kevin L. Danti, 339–66. Bethesda, MD: CDL Press, 1997.

Olyan, Saul M. *Friendship in Hebrew Bible*. New Haven: Yale University Press, 2017.

Peters, Kurtis. "Together in Guilt: David, Jonadab, and the Rape of Tamar." *Journal for the Study of the Old Testament* 45, no. 3 (2021): 309–19.

Probyn, Elspeth. *Carnal Appetites: FoodSexIdentities*. New York: Routledge, 2000.

Prohaska, Ariane, and Jeannine A. Gailey. "Achieving Masculinity Through Sexual Predation: The Case of Hogging." *Journal of Gender Studies* 19, no. 1 (2010): 13–25. doi:10.1080/09589230903525411.

Propp, William H. "Kinship in 2 Samuel 13." *The Catholic Biblical Quarterly* 55, no. 1 (1993): 39–53.

Rubin, Gayle S. "The Traffic in Women: Notes on the 'Political Economy' of Sex." In *The Second Wave: A Reader in Feminist Theory*, edited by Linda Nicholson, 27–62. New York: Routledge, 1997.

Rudman, Dominic. "Reliving the Rape of Tamar: Absalom's Revenge in 2 Samuel 13." *Old Testament Essays N.S.* 11, no. 2 (1998): 326–39.

Sanders, Seth. "Absalom's Audience (2 Samuel 15–19)." *Journal of Biblical Literature* 138, no. 3 (January 2019): 513–36. doi:10.15699/jbl.1383.2019.2891.

Sedgwick, Eve Kosofsky. *Between Men: English Literature and Male Homosocial Desire. Gender and Culture.* New York: Columbia University Press, 1985.

Stone, Ken. *Sex, Honor, and Power in the Deuteronomistic History.* Journal for the Study of the Old Testament Supplement Series 234. Sheffield: Sheffield Academic Press, 1996.

Stone, Ken. *Practicing Safer Texts: Food, Sex, and Bible in Queer Perspective.* London and New York: T&T Clark International, 2005.

Stone, Ken. "Marriage and Sexual Relations in the World of the Hebrew Bible." In *The Oxford Handbook of Theology, Sexuality, and Gender*, edited by Adrian Thatcher, 176–77. Oxford: Oxford University Press, 2015. doi:10.1093/oxfordhb/9780199664153.013.020.

Thiede, Barbara. *Male Friendship, Homosociality, and Women of the Hebrew Bible: Malignant Fraternities.* Routledge Studies in the Biblical World 5. London and New York: Routledge, 2022. doi:10.4324/9780429326226.

Tombs, David. "Abandonment, Rape, and Second Abandonment: Hannah Baker in *13 Reasons Why* and King David's Concubines in 2 Samuel 15–20." *The Shiloh Project: Rape Culture, Religion, and the Bible*, October 18, 2017. www.shilohproject.blog/abandonment-rape-and-second-abandonment-hannah-baker-in-13-reasons-why-and-king-davids-concubines-in-2-samuel-15-2/.

Trible, Phyllis. *Texts of Terror: Literary-Feminist Readings of Biblical Narratives.* Philadelphia: Fortress Press, 1984.

Van Dijk-Hemmes, Fokkelien. "Tamar and the Limits of Patriarchy: Between Rape and Seduction (2 Samuel 13 and Genesis 38)." In *Anti-Covenant: Counter-Reading Women's Lives in the Hebrew Bible*, edited by Mieke Bal, 135–56. Sheffield: Almond Press, 1989.

Van Selms, A. "The Origin of the Title 'The King's Friend'." *Journal of Near Eastern Studies* 16, no. 2 (April 1957): 118–23.

Washington, Harold C. "Violence and the Construction of Gender in the Hebrew Bible: A New Historicist Approach." *Biblical Interpretation* 5 (1997). 324–63.

Wilson, Stephen M. *Making Men: The Male Coming-of-Age Theme in the Hebrew Bible.* New York: Oxford University Press, 2015.

Wright, G.R.H. "Dumuzi at the Court of David." *Numen* 28, fasc. 1 (June 1981): 54–63.

Yancey Martin, Patricia, and Robert A. Hummer. "Fraternities and Rape on Campus." *Gender & Society* 3, no. 4 (December 1989): 457–73. doi:10.1177/089124389003004004.

2 The Taking, Trapping, and Raping of Women
Michal and Bathsheba

Introduction: Saul and David, Kings of Biblical Rape Culture

Men of the Hebrew Bible engage in sexual violence to negotiate power. Rape, perforce, becomes a predictable feature of its narratives. Rape is neither an exception nor an outlier.[1] It is a medium, a means for navigating rank, status, and authority. Male characters who hold the most power, be they divine or mortal, god or king, are not only protagonists in the rape culture of the Hebrew Bible, but also role models. In these narratives, the deity and his kings order the world by, in significant measure, showing how to take and rape women. Women and their bodies serve to enhance and protect divine and royal reputations, to accelerate or foil male competition, and to expedite displays of virility.

Michal and Bathsheba serve just such ends. The narratives in which they appear feature kings at the height of their power. But both King Saul and King David face challenges to their authority. Shame, humiliation, and honor will be key concerns for them and for the men they themselves demean. The network of men deployed in their service will inhabit all levels of court society, from servants to soldiers and courtiers to generals.

Biblical hegemonic masculinity, and the rape culture it undergirds, require collusion among men. Collusion occurs on multiple levels: biblical authors create voyeuristic scenes that engage the participation of the characters, their ancient audiences, and even modern readers. In the end, what we learn when we read of Michal and Bathsheba is that biblical rape culture depends, like any other, on the taking and raping of women as normalized behaviors. Sexual violence is a *premise*, not an outcome, of the competition for power, honor, and authority in biblical Israel.[2]

Michal: Bait—and Switched

The first time we meet Michal, Saul's second daughter, we learn that neither her desires nor access to her body can be separated from male agendas.[3]

The author makes this fact painfully clear in a single verse: "Now Michal daughter of Saul had fallen in love with David; and when this was reported to Saul, he was pleased" (1 Sam. 18:20). The author is less interested in Michal's love than in how her love can be leveraged. Saul's men can trade on some juicy gossip which will delight the king, who in turn believes he can exploit Michal's feelings for David (18:21). Scholars have noted that Michal is the only woman whose love for a man is explicitly stated.[4] The biblical author has a reason to indulge in describing a woman's love: it can be weaponized by one man against his rival.

Michal will continue to find herself the object in male competitions and intrigues. After she helps David escape her murderous father, Saul will marry her off to another man, perhaps to weaken David's claims to the throne, now that Saul's own son, Jonathan, has relinquished it.[5] By asserting his control over Michal and marrying her off to another man, Saul will also attempt to reassert his (dwindling) authority. David, in turn, will insist on reaffirming his right to Michal when he needs to cement his. Michal's story becomes a patchwork of transactions among men. She is given by her father, taken by David, given away a second time to Paltiel, retaken by David and, in the end, cast aside again (1 Sam. 18:20–27; 1 Sam. 25:44; 2 Sam. 3:14–15; 2 Sam. 6:23). Other men will play their parts as messengers, courtiers, advisors. A company of men will negotiate how Michal is used, objectified, and demeaned.

When we meet Michal, King Saul ought to be at the height of his power. He has fathered at least five children and may already have collected a number of women.[6] Nevertheless, cracks are emerging. The first king of Israel has made significant mistakes, according to both Samuel and Yhwh.[7] Goliath, who terrified the Israelites, was not done away with by Israel's warrior king but by a brash shepherd boy. Still, Saul has men to command, courtiers to attend to his needs, a brave son and heir, a just-arrived beautiful young champion to serve him, and women to prove his prowess. Saul may be a flawed and vulnerable king, but he has, at this point in the story, control of crown and throne.

Young David will soon threaten all he has. In 1 Samuel 18, the biblical author takes just eight verses to show how David wins the love and admiration of the nation. He is celebrated as the quintessential hero who has killed and bested the enemy, led his soldiers in every charge, and displayed the fearlessness of a true warrior. Saul and Jonathan, too, love David, who pleases the troops he leads and the men of Saul's court. He is noticed, admired, and loved.

His success shames the king, whose job description David fills and exceeds. According to the Israelites, kings, not their generals, march out before the troops (1 Sam. 8:20). It is David who wins the acclaim and adoration of the Israelites for acting as the king should. But it is not only the men whose hearts David wins. David makes a final conquest, one that leads to Saul's utter humiliation. Upon his return from battle against the Philistines, the women of all the towns of Israel come out—ostensibly—to greet King Saul (1 Sam. 18:6). What happens, however, is a crushing public embarrassment. The women dance and sing, and the words to their song are, for the king, a gut-level punch: "Saul has slain his thousands; David, his tens of thousands!" (18:7).

The women's response is particularly pertinent; dancing has sexual signification in the Hebrew Bible. The term in this verse (חול) is associated both with turning and with writhing while giving birth (Isa. 13:8, 26:17; Mic. 4:10; Jer. 4:31).[8] The association between dancing women and fertility is obvious, and the implications here are devastating. David has, in effect, acquired the bodies of all the women of Israel for his viewing pleasure. Women are turning, perhaps even writhing, before their new champion. David is the virile hero. Saul is the mortified and emasculated king. He knows how serious the women's betrayal is: "To David they have given tens of thousands, and to me they have given thousands. All that he lacks is the kingship!" (1 Sam. 18:8). From that day on, the biblical author tells us, "Saul kept a jealous eye on David" (18:9).

A king who loses control over women's bodies loses honor, reputation, and social currency—all those things that give him the authority to be king in the first place. How does Saul attempt to reclaim all three? Rejected by Israel's women, he attempts to use his own women to facilitate the death of his competitor. He first offers David his eldest daughter Merab, but quickly reneges on that offer. Perhaps his eldest is too great a prize, permitting David to stand too near the throne. Saul marries Merab off to another (less threatening) man instead (1 Sam. 18:19).

Saul's courtiers are well aware that the king is both jealous and afraid of his new general. Some surely witnessed or heard about Saul physically attacking David while he was playing his lyre for the king (1 Sam. 18:10–11). Twice, Saul throws his spear at the young musician. Twice he misses. The contest for the future of Israel is tied to sexualized aggression against men too: Saul attempts to penetrate David with the manliest weapon he has. His failed attempt to penetrate David's body with his spear will be followed by attempts to control him through the body of a woman.

Perhaps Saul's courtiers are currying favor with the king when they report to him that Michal has fallen in love with David (1 Sam. 18:20). Perhaps they anticipate exactly what Saul will do, which is to exult in the news. If they know their king, they know his mind. "I will give her to him," Saul thinks, "and she can serve as a snare for him, so that the Philistines may kill him" (18:20–21). Saul suggests marriage to David yet again; he can become his son-in-law with "the second one" (18:21). Michal is David's consolation prize and Saul's weapon—or so he thinks.

The sexual display by the Israelite women for David's benefit threatens Saul. In return, Saul will use sexual access to Michal to compromise and threaten David. Giving David access to and ownership of Michal's body will, Saul hopes, make David vulnerable, or at least acquiescent. David will have to go on doing battle for his king and continue to risk his life at the front of the troops. His death, Saul imagines, is inevitable. Best of all, Saul will bear no guilt when it occurs.[9]

Scholars have long noted how male-male competition leads to handing Michal from one man to another: "In the case of Michal," J. Cheryl Exum writes, "the issue is *male rivalry*, where woman is frequently victim" (2016b, 35; italics original).[10] But Michal will not merely be traded from man to man; she will be at the center of a wide network of men who will discuss her fate, serve as negotiators and colluders, and manage sexual access to her body.

Saul sets out to deploy all his men to ensnare David. Saul's men are to tell David how fond the king is of him and to remind him how well loved he is by the king's courtiers. Why not become the king's son-in-law (1 Sam. 18:22)? David responds as he did when he was offered Merab, demurring and declaring his unworthiness (18:23). The courtiers report back to Saul, who baits the trap by offering David an opportunity to demonstrate his virility. Saul sets a task he assumes must end in David's death, demanding he produce one hundred Philistine foreskins for Michal's bride price. But David does *not* die in the attempt (18:25). He comes back to court before Saul's deadline, laying *two hundred* foreskins before the king (18:26–27). David is granted Michal. It cannot be otherwise. David has proven he has what it takes to be an ideal warrior and the son-in-law of the king. He has feminized his enemy in a kind of mass castration and, by doing so, broadcasted his potency and might. Saul's plans are not merely foiled: David has thoroughly shown up the king of all Israel before his own court.

Saul is forced to confront reality: he cannot leverage Michal's love for David to engineer his rival's death. The young general is backed by Yhwh (1 Sam. 18:28). The deity's attraction for the handsome young shepherd boy is obvious. When David shows his attractive self before Samuel, his beauty is described and extolled (1 Sam. 16:12), and divine attention follows.[11] Yhwh makes his own affections clear in a divine penetrative act once David is oiled up. His spirit rushes into David (ותצלח רוח יהוה אל דוד) and remains there, from that day forward (16:13).[12]

Translations do not typically convey the sexualized language at work. They describe the deity's spirit as one which "possesses" or "grips" the human object of the deity's attentions. But the term used here, *tzalakh* (צלח), connotes a marked degree of force, as Baruch Levine points out (2009, 35–36), and a penetrative act. *Tzalach* can be translated as "to split," "to force entry," or "to penetrate." The latter is particularly likely when either the preposition *al* (על) or *el* (אל) is used before the verb (Koehler and Baumgartner 2001, 1026).[13] Yhwh has laid claim to David and to his body. David lays claim to Yhwh in turn, calling on his backer and boasting to Goliath that the Israelite deity will deliver the giant into his hands (1 Sam. 17:46). Yhwh does.

Saul has reason to worry. A king must maintain his honor and control; his subordinates must procure his wishes and follow his commands. Saul now attempts to recruit both son and servants, urging them to kill David for him (1 Sam. 19:1). Instead, Jonathan makes the case for the man he loves, and for two verses all seems well (19:4–7). But David wins again against the Philistines. His sponsor, Yhwh, adds insult to injury by sending his evil spirit into Saul again (19:8–9). Saul has to prove himself the man and launches a second attack on David (19:10).

When that attempt fails, Saul enlists his servants and courtiers (1 Sam. 19:11).[14] The men of Saul's court may admire, even love, David, but they have not yet abandoned their king. Saul sends messengers to his son-in-law's home, instructing them to, in effect, put him under house arrest. They are to kill him at dawn (19:11). As Saul attempts yet again to do away with David, Michal will once again be encircled by a company of men who hope to use her for their own ends.

Michal warns David: he must run for his life (1 Sam. 19:11). The biblical author does not tell us why Michal helps David escape; her love for her husband may still be unwavering. Or, perhaps, she is telling the truth when she later tells her father that David threatened to kill her if she didn't abet his escape (19:17). Michal is trapped in the house with David and may have reason to fear for her own safety. In the Hebrew Bible, when men come to a house to kill or abuse men, women in the house are bartered, even offered to the men outside (Gen. 19:8; Judg. 19:24). Walls cannot protect women; their safety is dependent on the men who live inside (and outside) their home. Michal is caught between men in a life-or-death contest. Saul's messengers are planning to kill a man who is well-known as the fiercest of warriors. A bloody encounter awaits.

A network of men with male agendas and male demands encircles Michal. She must answer to David's needs, one way or another. She must navigate the danger posed by the executioners Saul has sent to kill David by fooling them and buying time (1 Sam. 19:12). The messengers themselves have something to fear from a young warrior who slices and dices

Philistines like so much produce. Saul's executioners respond to Michal's claim that David is sick in bed not by verifying it for themselves, but, almost comically, by rushing back to the king for further instruction. They return to David's house to find that Michal has dressed up an idol to mimic her husband asleep in his bed.

The scheme is aborted; once again, Saul has been made to look a fool, and his men along with him. Every one of Saul's failed attempts on David's life only demonstrates that the first king of Israel is a flop, one whose masculinity and honor cannot be maintained or protected, much less admired. Saul's fumbles, and those of his men, expose the failure of his networks, of his subordinates, and, above all, of his own manly strength. In the end, neither Saul nor his sons will be able to use Michal to advance their own agendas. To take a woman, even to rape a woman, requires the successful exercise of power and control. It will be left to David and *his* men to demonstrate how to do both.

By this time, Michal has been given by her father, taken by David, and isolated and left behind by both. The men of the court have been witnesses and collaborators at every step. David will make no effort to return for her, and her father will send her off to be taken by yet another man. Michal all but disappears from the narrative, out of sight and out of mind. Her dismissal is so thorough that she only deserves mention as a kind of afterthought once David acquires more women—Ahinoam of Jezreel and Abigail, whom he takes from her foolish husband Nabal (1 Sam. 25:44).[15]

Michal is essentially forgotten for the rest of the first Book of Samuel. David is busy consolidating resources and acquiring other women. In 2 Samuel 1, he learns that Saul and Jonathan have died in battle. The narrator announces that David's house is growing stronger while Saul's is growing weaker (2 Sam. 3:1) and provides evidence of David's virility and potency: he has acquired half a dozen wives and sired as many sons (3:2). David demonstrates his vigor on fields of battle and in his bedrooms in Hebron. But Michal is still a prize worth having. She represents David's ties to the dead king of Israel. He will enhance his own claims by having Saul's daughter at his own side once again.

The opening for David's move comes from Abner, first cousin to Saul and general of Saul's troops from the outset of his kingship (1 Sam. 14:50). Abner is important to Saul's story; his first mention immediately follows the list of Saul's children and heirs (14:49). It is Abner who identifies David to Saul after the killing of Goliath.[16] And it is Abner whom David challenges by stealing Saul's spear and water jug while the king is sleeping. Abner was key to advising and protecting the first king of Israel; he will become key to the second king too.

After the death of Saul, Abner remains loyal to Saul's descendants. He supports Saul's second son, Ish-bosheth, making him king over the northern regions of Israel (2 Sam. 2:8). Abner, then, is not only the right-hand man of Saul, he also becomes, after Saul's death, a kingmaker. His military prowess and political power grow by leaps and bounds. Abner was a powerhouse in the House of Saul and is now enhancing his ability to shape events. In 2 Samuel 3:6, we read that Abner is making himself strong in Saul's house (היה מתחזק בבית שאול). The operative word here, *mitchazeyk*, comes from a root that means "to seize" (חזק) and appears in contexts of sexual violence (e.g., Deut. 22:25, 28; Judg. 19:25; 2 Sam. 13:14). Men make themselves strong by defeating their enemies and by taking and raping women.[17]

Abner has certainly proven himself capable of the former during his years of service to Saul. In the next verse he demonstrates his ability to do the latter, and in a way that brazenly challenges the man whom he himself has just made king. Saul, we are told, had a *pilegesh* named Rizpah.[18] After Saul's death, Abner takes her for his sexual use (2 Sam. 3:7). The new king, Saul's second son Ish-bosheth, is affronted. He challenges Abner's right to Rizpah (3:7).[19] A man proves his masculinity, or "makes himself strong," by killing his enemies, humiliating them, taking women, and fathering sons. We have just read of Abner's military prowess and his killing of Joab's brother Asahel in 2 Samuel 2. Here, just after learning of David's growing strength and sexual prowess, we learn of Abner's (3:2–7).

Some scholars suggest that Abner is himself making a play for the throne by taking the former king's concubine. Ken Stone argues, however, that since Abner has just crowned Ish-bosheth, it is more likely that the episode simply reveals the nature of male contests in the Hebrew Bible, contests in which men test one another's performance of masculinity. The winner is the one who controls access to a woman's body (1996, 89). "The result of the quarrel," as Stone writes, "is a series of distinctly political facts" (86).

If Stone is correct, Abner is challenging Ish-bosheth, forcing him to prove whether he is man enough to be king. Technically, Ish-bosheth is in control of who has sexual access to his father's former *pilegesh*. Practically, he is obviously not in charge. From Ish-bosheth's perspective, Abner has demeaned his royal authority and insulted his honor by taking Rizpah for himself. From Abner's point of view, Ish-bosheth doesn't have what it takes to deserve his support. He will change allegiances. He sends messengers to David suggesting a pact (2 Sam. 3:12). Despite years of loyalty to Saul's house, Abner would now rather become David's strongman than continue to support a weak and fearful pretender (3:11).

This is a golden opportunity for David, and he takes full advantage of it. He is amenable to a pact, but on one condition: Abner must bring him Michal (2 Sam. 3:13). In a dramatic *coup de grâce*, David indirectly tells

Ish-bosheth, too, just who calls the shots. He sends men to deliver his message (3:14): "Give me my wife Michal," he commands, "who I paid for with 100 foreskins" (תנה את אשתי את מיכל אשר ארשתי לי במאה ערלות פלשתים).
David reminds Ish-bosheth what a real man does to his enemies.

When men clash, women are their pawns. During this episode, Abner challenges Ish-bosheth's honor and rights by taking Rizpah for his own. David, in turn, demands his first wife back by reminding Saul's son how willing he is to inflict sexual humiliation on men who stand in his way. Michal, a woman who has been traded and taken twice, will now be traded for a third time. Once again, a strongman and warrior stands at the side of the king, colludes in the management of a woman's body, and oversees her transfer. Such male alliances were behind Amnon's rape of Tamar and Absalom's rape of David's *pilagshim*, too.

Michal is taken from a man who bewails her loss. Paltiel, her second husband, follows behind her, weeping, until Abner orders him to turn back (2 Sam. 3:16). David is, indeed, proving who should be king after Saul: the man who can take women from other men; the man who can humiliate the men he defeats; the man whose power and reach attracts men who are themselves proven warriors and leaders. Abner has put his money on the right horse. He consolidates his win by convincing the elders of Israel and Saul's own tribe, the Benjaminites, to throw their allegiance behind David (3:17–18).

All that remains is a minor clean-up operation. Joab, David's nephew and commander of his army, is jealous of Abner and takes out his competition by nefariously murdering Abner at the gates of Hebron (3:27). Two of Ish-bosheth's company commanders attempt to curry favor with David by murdering Ish-bosheth and bringing his head to Hebron (2 Sam. 4:5–8). David is crowned king, captures Jerusalem, and renames the stronghold the City of David (5:9), building a palace with King Hiram's help (5:11). Unsurprisingly, the biblical author announces that David expands his harem again, taking more *pilagshim* and more wives in Jerusalem. He has work to do, and he does it, siring more sons (5:13–16) and fighting more Philistines (5:17–25).

Upon his first arrival at Saul's court,[20] back when he was a youth, David finds all other Israelites running in fear at the mere sight of Goliath; David, however, advances on the giant and brazenly announces his inevitable demise (1 Sam. 17:45–47). He doubles the drama when it comes to the purchase of Michal, bringing twice the number of Philistine foreskins to count out before King Saul (18:27). After David's kingship is consolidated, we should expect a theatrical scene of triumph when he takes the Ark of the Covenant back from the defeated Philistines. We get one.

Earlier, it was all the women of Israel who danced in celebration and sang David's praises, turning and writhing in a communal and ecstatic act of hero worship. Now it will be David himself who dances in an exhibitionist frenzy. As Theodore W. Jennings notes, David is dressed in an ephod, a linen apron of sorts that both loosely covers and draws attention to his genitals (2005, 45). He whirls before Yhwh with such force that he exposes himself to all those present.[21] He dances before divine junk too, because, as Jennings argues, both the divine ephod and the Ark of the Covenant "disguise and disclose the phallic potency of Adonai" (47). "The ark," he adds, "before which David dances is the sheathed phallus of his lover" (47).[22] It is important to note that the verb used to describe David's dancing (כרר) evokes a male-only setting; its etymological origins can be found describing battle maneuvers. It is never used in the Hebrew Bible to denote women's dancing. This is a man dancing for his man.

The passage is awash with sexual imagery. The biblical author describes Michal watching from a window,[23] noting David's display and disdaining him for it. Perhaps Michal is aware that she has repeatedly lost David to the love of men; perhaps she is envious (Jennings 2005, 40). More likely, the male biblical author wants to portray her as carping and jealous. David triumphs. His dance, he tells her, is for the sake of Yhwh, who has clearly chosen him over her father (2 Sam. 6:21). Michal may believe David cannot win respect from the slave girls subjected to his indecent exposure; he says otherwise. If he danced with more abandon, they would still honor him (6:22). Just as the women of Israel once honored him with the erotic display of their dancing bodies, they will honor *his* erotic display before them. The feelings are mutual.

David's men have no reason to complain about their king's display of virility.[24] In a world in which men perform their power, authority, status, and virility through the sexual use of women, homoerotic displays of sexuality are rewarded. This is a fantasy scene for the biblical writer and for his male audience. A man dances, turns, and exposes himself—and the biblical author wants to make sure that the men in his audience know that Israel's women love it.[25]

David's homoerotic display on behalf of Yhwh elicits heterosexual enjoyment. Yhwh is treated to his man's ecstatic dance, and Israelite women are assumed to enjoy the show. Israelite men can be imagined taking vicarious pleasure in either aspect of David's performance of a virile, powerful masculinity. The king's dance appeals to all Israel, divine or mortal, male or female. The biblical audience—and the modern one—experience each commanding move David makes, each thrill he provides. Male fraternities support and enjoy male displays of sexual prowess.

We can expect exactly what happens next in this narrative—a female voice who dares to challenge such masculine displays will be cast as a disrespectful shrew and punished for criticizing a man. Michal will never again be the recipient of David's sexual attentions. To her dying day, the daughter of Saul will have no child (2 Sam. 6:23).[26] The death knell sounded here is complete. Michal, who has been given and taken, abandoned, given and taken again, is abandoned a final time. Courtiers, messengers, generals, kings—brothers and fathers and husbands: they have all played a part in passing her from one location to the next, from one man to the next. It is their competitions for power, their need for ascendancy, that the narrative is at pains to describe. Like David's *pilagshim*, Michal is left to await her death.

Biblical rape culture depicts a world in which men control women's sexuality. They decide who can access it, and when. In the Hebrew Bible, to "take" women (לקח) means to "go into" them (בוא), to penetrate them (e.g., Genesis 38:2).[27] Biblical rape culture rests on the assumption that women have nothing to say about whether their bodies can be penetrated. Every woman of the Hebrew Bible belongs to a man, whether that be Yhwh, his chosen kings, his patriarchs or prophets, Israelite generals, soldiers, or farmers. Michal lives in a rape culture, and her story demonstrates what that rape culture will mean for her body; she is owned, exchanged, and silenced—ultimately, to death.[28]

Bathsheba

What happens to both Michal and Bathsheba is not, ultimately, about either woman. The biblical author is telling a man's story to a male audience. Male honor, prestige, and authority are his subject. Women and their bodies serve male agendas, male "needs," and male desires. We learn from both narratives how women's bodies serve as instruments for reestablishing dominance when a leader feels challenged or shamed. When the women of Israel compare David's military successes to Saul's, Israel's first king uses his daughter Michal to entrap David and attempt to ensure his demise. When King Hanun of Ammon shames David's messengers publicly (2 Sam. 10:4), David responds by sending his general Joab to besiege the Ammonite capital while he remains in Jerusalem to ogle, take, and rape Bathsheba (11:1-4). Both Michal and Bathsheba are tools; their bodies used by men to assert or restore their sovereignty.

In biblical texts the taking of women is a permission slip for the raping of women. Nowhere is this more apparent than in 2 Samuel 11, a chapter that recounts how David sees, discovers, takes, and rapes the wife of one of his own generals. The opening of this chapter demonstrates a chilling combination of male calculation, initiative, and action, just as we witness two chapters later, when Jonadab and Amnon plot the taking and raping of Tamar in a mere five verses.

Bathsheba, like Michal, will have her body, her movements, and her existence subordinated to male contests for power. The rape of Bathsheba will involve an exhibitionist display of power that will lead to murder, not only of Uriah but of other men who fight on behalf of the king.[29] Again, a host of men will be involved from the start; again, we will see that the taking and raping of women functions as a test and as proof of a man's might. As we know from the rapes of Tamar and the *pilagshim*, male battles over the future of Israel are tied to sexualized aggression, the use of women's bodies, and the collusion of a company of men.

By 2 Samuel 11, David appears at the zenith of his power. He has conquered Jerusalem, acquired wives and concubines, and fathered many sons (2 Sam. 4–5). He has retaken the Ark of the Covenant and brought it to the City of David (6). He has subdued the Philistines and defeated the Moabites, literally measuring out who will live and who will die and subsequently enslaving the survivors (8:2). King Hadadezer of Zobab is defeated, and when the Arameans try to rescue him, they, too, are struck down and forced into servitude (8:3–6). The Edomites share their fate (8:14). Indeed, Yhwh gives David victory wherever he goes (8:6), and each of his triumphs demonstrates his right and his ability to humiliate and demean his enemies. In the next chapter, David makes sure the sole survivor of the House of Saul, Jonathan's crippled son Mephibosheth, is brought to his court as his dependent (9:1–10).

After so much success, David can afford to be magnanimous. When Nahash, the king of Ammon, dies, David sends messengers to his son Hanun with condolences (2 Sam. 10:2). It may seem strange that David boasts of a friendly relationship with a king who once threatened to gouge out the right eye of every man of Jabesh-gilead (1 Sam. 11:2). But one violent king can respect another and choose to ally with a former enemy. In any case, the Ammonites, who have doubtless heard of David's recent conquests, suspect David's courtiers of nefarious motives. They tell their king that David has sent his messengers to spy out the city and prepare another Israelite military victory (2 Sam. 10:3). Hanun believes them. Before David can possibly humiliate him, Hanun publicly shames David's messengers. He clips off one side of their beards (10:4). Beards symbolize virility and masculine honor.[30] Hanun has stripped both from David's men. Then, he orders their garments cut away so that their buttocks are exposed (10:4). Naturally, David does not welcome his men home. They have been stripped and emasculated. Their public appearance would demonstrate his own loss of power and loss of face. He orders them to stay in Jericho until their beards grow back (10:5). The Ammonites hire Aramean troops for the battle they expect David to wage, and war ensues.

Sara Koenig notes that "the whole narrative of the Ammonite war is set against a challenge to David's masculinity through his envoys" (2015, 499).[31] David's men have been feminized, even symbolically castrated.

David's defeat of the Aramean mercenaries hired by Hanun provides a first step in regaining his honor and proving his masculine bona fides. David has a time-worn path available to him to redeem his honor; he could go out and conquer his opponent on his own. But he does not lead the charge against Hanun. Instead, he stays in Jerusalem and sends Joab in his place (2 Sam. 11:1). Perhaps he intends to humiliate Hanun by sending the signal that the Ammonite king is too lowly to be worth David's while. But another way that powerful men react to being shamed is to use a woman's bodies as a proxy. When David shames Saul by winning every battle, gaining loyalty and love from the troops, and receiving a display of female exuberance that dismisses Saul's own military achievements, Saul begins casting about for ways to reassert his control. Saul uses his own authority over Michal's body in an attempt to regain his authority and rank. Now, when David's honor has been impugned, he too engages in a public display of *his* authority over a woman's body.

It is the springtime, a time when kings go out to fight. David has defeated Ammonite mercenaries but sends Joab out to engage the Ammonites (2 Sam. 11:1). The king remains in Jerusalem, indulging in royal naps and kingly strolls around the palace. Late one afternoon he arises from his couch and takes a walk on the roof. His eyes alight on Bathsheba bathing (11:2). The king's interest is piqued; he wants information. Someone is sent to make inquiries. "A woman is touching herself," writes Exum, "and a man is watching. The viewing is one-sided, giving him the advantage and the position of power: he sees her but she does not see him" (2012, 34). We should not, however, imagine that David watches alone. One of David's servants stands with him. At least *two* men are watching a woman touch herself.[32]

The servant identifies the beautiful woman as Bathsheba, the daughter of Eliam and the wife of Uriah the Hittite (2 Sam. 11:3). The Hebrew text is formulated as a question: "Is that not Bathsheba?" (הלוא זאת בת שבע).[33] Clearly, Uriah's home is nearby. Is the male biblical author inviting his audience to imagine that men watching Bathsheba is a recurring event among palace servants or courtiers?

Some scholars suggest that Bathsheba enticed the king with an exhibitionist display.[34] But blaming Bathsheba for the king's ogling from high above—David is standing on the roof of his palace, after all—aligns with the premises of rape culture, which assume that women are asking for the sexual attention, even sexual violence, that men force upon them.[35] And there is no indication that Bathsheba is attempting to seduce the king: the action is all David's (Stone 1996, 97).[36] Bathsheba is never criticized for what happened either. Only David is called to account (2 Sam. 12:9). The biblical author is far less interested in blaming Bathsheba than he is in using her to excite his male biblical audience. The biblical audience (and the modern one) are being presented with a well-worn and exciting trope: a woman is engaged in intimate acts, unaware that she is being watched.[37] Scenes which make a woman an unwitting performer for male heterosexual fantasies are popular for a reason: they create opportunities for shared sexual experience among viewers, even if only vicariously. Here, the viewers not only include male characters in the text, they include the male author, his biblical audience, and generations of readers that follow. There is a particularly illicit pleasure in stripping away a woman's clothing without her knowledge.[38]

And, as we have seen in Chapter 1, for a king (or prince) to show off his sexual prowess is a spectacle that can be enjoyed vicariously by other men. Despite scholarly and exegetical attempts to make Bathsheba the exhibitionist in this story, it is the king who deserves to be accused. David shows off his virility (again) and engages in exhibitionist display (again).

Certainly, David and one of his men are sharing the experience. And just as certainly, one or two of his men are now well aware of the king's interest in Bathsheba. But taking the wife of a man is something they leave to the king; male servants might have the opportunity and power to ogle, but their privilege ends there. It is the king who may have any woman he desires sent to his rooms for his sexual use. Such sexual excess on the part of kings is found elsewhere in the Hebrew Bible: Solomon, after all, had seven hundred royal wives and three hundred *pilagshim* to send for at will (1 Kings 11:3), and Ahasuerus had young and beautiful virgins from every province brought to him to sample (Esther 2:2).

Once he discovers who Bathsheba is, David sends men to fetch her. None of this happens in the dark of night or in secrecy, as scholars have noted (Frymer-Kensky 2002, 146). Still, scholars miss the masculine display that is going on. Before his courtiers and servants, David has established his interest in a woman who belongs to one of his men—one of his thirty intimate soldier-companions, in fact (2 Sam. 23:34). He has discussed her and watched her with at least one man, who himself may already have known how and when to observe Bathsheba. He has sent men to fetch her. He has displayed before his servants and courtiers just how good it is to be the king.[39]

Long ago, all the women of Israel came out to dance before David, to demonstrate to whom they belonged. David himself danced before all Israel, flaunting his virility in the most obvious terms. He has claimed the might to control every woman, from maidservants to princesses to other men's wives. Every man involved must know and imagine what the king is about; every man involved can see the scene unfolding. David might not rape Bathsheba before his men's eyes as his son Absalom rapes his father's *pilagshim* (2 Sam. 16:22). But he will be raping her in their minds' eyes. It is nothing short of an exhibitionist display of masculine might and virility on the king's part. And no man will stop him, even though taking another man's wife is considered "the great sin."[40] Power matters. In biblical rape culture, the deity himself announces that he hands women from one man to another (2 Sam. 12:8); why shouldn't a divinely appointed king be able to follow suit?

Like Bathsheba, Michal was first encircled: by her father, King Saul, his courtiers, and servants. Later, she is encircled by David, Abner, and her brother Ish-bosheth. In the first four verses of her story, Bathsheba will be encircled by King David, his courtiers, and servants, all of whom collude and collaborate to make it possible for David to take her and rape her. Later, Joab will help deal with the fall-out. A company of men surrounds Bathsheba, too, at every step.

In quick succession, we learn that David has sent out his messengers (וישלח דוד מלאכים) and that he took her (ויקחה). Bathsheba "came to him" (ותבוא אליו), and he lay with her (וישכב עמה). David is the subject of three of these clauses (2 Sam. 11:4). Bathsheba, by contrast, is the direct or indirect object. The one exception, which describes her coming to David, is suspect. As scholars have noted, that phrase is superfluous, interrupting the flow of the verse.[41] This is, quite possibly, the reason why it is wholly omitted in the Septuagint.[42] Assuming the phrase "and she came to him" was *not* an editorial insertion but "original" to the narrative[43] should not, however, lead to the conclusion that Bathsheba was a willing participant. There is no evidence that she knew what David wanted.[44] Moreover, kings who summon are the ones who hold power, not the women they order to attend them. This is amply demonstrated in the Book of Esther, where the young and beautiful virgins who are brought to Ahasuerus' palace live lives that are entirely dependent on the king's grace (Esther 2:2–4). Vashti, who refuses to come at the king's command, is cast out and replaced as queen (Esther 1:19). As Anne Létourneau writes, "Bathsheba's existence now depends on the king's desire. Royal authority and the violent control it allows determine her situation and choices . . . Bathsheba, as a good royal subject, has to walk" (2018, 80).

The terminology deployed in this verse signifies both the use of force and what is forbidden. When the Hebrew root for lying down, *shachav* (שכב), is used in connection with a sexual encounter, the relationship it describes is illicit.[45] The term for taking, *lakach* (לקח), can mean to "seize," "capture," and "grasp" and is often employed to indicate the use of force. When the biblical authors use *lakach* without the Hebrew term for "a woman," we are encountering a base act (Andruska 2017, 105–6).[46] Exum states simply: "He sent, he took, and he lay: the verbs signify control and acquisition" (2012, 29).[47] Assuming that Bathsheba was the victim of force also explains why the text never blames her. This is significant. Biblical texts are quick to blame women, and even execute them for presumably committing adultery (Deut. 22:22–24).

David has succeeded. He has taken Bathsheba into his rooms. Unlike Amnon, who thought it impossible "to do" anything to his sister—and he was clearly wrong about that—David never has to consider whether he has the right to have Bathsheba brought to him for his sexual use. Neither do any of his men see any reason to question his actions. Rape cultures, whether actual or literary, rely on male collusion where the control of women's bodies is concerned. And so, Bathsheba washes, then returns home. Perhaps the author is enjoying yet another moment of voyeuristic intimacy. For women who have been raped, the scene is likely a painful one. Bathsheba is doing what women so frequently do first after they have been assaulted: wash their bodies in an attempt to feel "clean" again after having been violated.[48]

Bathsheba becomes pregnant and tells David so in the briefest of messages (2 Sam. 11:5). It takes just two words to inform him (הרה אנכי), but the salient words in this verse are not limited to what they translate: "I am pregnant." Bathsheba cannot and does not go back to the palace herself. Instead, she sends someone to David with her message (ותשלח ותגד). We do not know who carries this explosive information to the king, whether one of his servants or one of hers. Most likely, yet another man has joined the narrative.[49] We cannot be sure how many messengers, in the end, must be deployed before someone tells David of his impending fatherhood.

The entire narrative features men sent hither and yon, from those sent to inquire who was bathing before David's peeping eyes to those who were sent to fetch Bathsheba, to whoever was sent to inform David of Bathsheba's pregnancy. Court intrigue was part and parcel of Saul's court, too. David sends out yet another servant—this time, a messenger to Joab with instructions to direct Bathsheba's husband Uriah to head home to Jerusalem (2 Sam. 11:6).

David will have to accomplish an important task. Perhaps all his courtiers and men will accept his taking and raping of Uriah's wife, but Uriah may not be so inclined. Bathsheba's pregnancy raises the stakes. The king will have to find a way to make Uriah believe the child is his, or else do away with Uriah altogether. For his part, David has had Bathsheba and doesn't need her again. He will, therefore, do his best to make sure Uriah takes her. Michal, too, was passed from David to Paltiel, when she no longer served her purpose in Saul's eyes. Women's bodies are men's objects to use and to discard as they please.

Saul tried to control David through the sexual use of a woman. David will now try to control Uriah through the sexual use of a woman. A man who displays his sexual prowess for others to admire will not be above encouraging and vicariously participating in the sexuality of others. David's first attempts to do just that are not subtle. When Uriah arrives, David engages him in small talk, asking about the welfare of his general, Joab, and his men (2 Sam. 11:7).[50] Then the king issues a direct command: "Go down to your house," he says, "and bathe your feet" (11:8).

Scholars often note that the word for "foot" (רגל) is a biblical euphemism for the male member. Such uses can be found in both narrative and in prophetic texts (e.g., Exod. 4:25; Ruth 3:8; Isa. 6:2; 7:20).[51] Crude references to male anatomy are hardly unknown in the Hebrew Bible. Indeed, they reflect the rape culture it depicts, one which equates the male member with power and authority and measures the size of the former to indicate the latter (1 Kings 12:10). In 2 Samuel 11:8 David has effectively commanded Uriah to bathe his member in his wife, hoping to obscure the fact that she was made pregnant by the king, rather than by her husband. The king is encouraging (and sharing) a vision of a sexually receptive wife waiting at home for her husband.[52] David sweetens the deal by sending another messenger after Uriah with a gift, perhaps delicacies from the court kitchen (2 Sam. 11:8). Food and sex go together, as we see when Tamar is made to mix, knead, shape, and bake pastries for Amnon before a host of male onlookers—just minutes before he rapes her.[53]

There is no doubt that Uriah knows exactly what David intends. Possibly, he has heard that his wife was brought to the palace; for all we know, he could have found out about her pregnancy. Bathsheba's summons to the palace happened in the open; her pregnancy, meanwhile, was disclosed to at least one person other than the king. Uriah does not take the bait. Instead, he sleeps at the entrance to the palace (2 Sam. 11:10). He is not alone; the biblical author tells us explicitly that Uriah beds down together with "all the servants of his lord" (כל עבדי אדניו). Surely, these men know that Uriah's choice *not* to visit his wife is deliberate, even calculated. Some may have been among those David sent to Uriah's house, or maybe they simply observed servants heading that way, laden with gifts. Surely, a number of David's men had some inkling of the plot, for they immediately report back to David (ויגדו לדוד) that Uriah did not go home (11:10). When David questions Uriah about the matter, Uriah responds in stalwart and soldierly style: "How can I go home and eat and drink and sleep with my wife? As you live, by your very life, I will not do this!" (11:11).[54] There might have been some scenario in which David and Uriah could have enjoyed sharing the fantasy of Bathsheba in a sexually available posture.[55] But not here. To share a woman involves assent on both men's sides. David took Bathsheba without such assent from Uriah. Uriah will not be urged on to have sex with his wife by the very man who has cuckolded him.

David tries once more. He insists that Uriah stay another day and wines and dines him until he is drunk (2 Sam. 11:13). Alcohol does away with inhibitions, and perhaps a merry Uriah will want to be merry with his wife. But this plan, too, does not meet with success.[56] Again, Uriah goes down to sleep with the officers. Bathsheba never sees him, much less sleeps with him.

David had sent for Bathsheba so that he could use her sexually. David sends for Uriah so that *he* can use Bathsheba sexually. The biblical author and his male audience have had ample opportunity to imagine Bathsheba being subjected to sexual use by more than one man. Sharing women's bodies among men, whether in one's imagination or in literary reality, is a feature of the Hebrew Bible and of the rape culture it describes. Such cultures depend on assuring men of their "right" to apportion who uses a woman and in what way.

How many men now encircle Bathsheba? David, his servants and courtiers, Uriah, Joab, royal officers . . . we might ask, who *isn't* in the know? Who hasn't been, or won't be, engaged to send or deliver messages? Who doesn't get involved in the efforts to make the story end well for David? The tale we read is, as always, about power and about the potential challenges that men in authority face. As David once challenged Saul as the young and brave general whose military prowess everyone admired, so Uriah challenges David as the humble soldier whose only thought is for his men and his own superior, Joab. How can he possibly sleep with his wife, he asks, when Yhwh's Ark, all the men of Israel and Judah, and Joab and David's own officers are camping in the field, fighting the king's battles (2 Sam. 11:11)?

David will succeed where Saul failed, for David's plans do not rely on chance. Uriah will not be sent out to face the enemy merely in the hope that he will be cut down. David will make sure that there can be no other outcome. He writes out his commands, and Uriah carries the instructions for his own death to Joab.[57] David's plan is straightforward: Uriah is to be placed in the front line where the fighting is fiercest; Joab should order the other men to fall back and leave Uriah to be slaughtered (2 Sam. 11:15). As Abner facilitated the taking of Michal from Paltiel, Joab now facilitates David's ability to take Bathsheba from Uriah. David's homosocial bonds are strengthened in both cases; the men David tasks with ugly jobs can assume they have cemented their relationship with the king and have raised their own status *vis-à-vis* other men. Given the nature of biblical hegemonic masculinity, it should not be surprising that both meet a humiliating end (2 Sam. 3:27; 1 Kings 2:34). Supporting David (or any king) is a dangerous affair.

Joab is not willing, however, to make Uriah's execution so obvious. David's strategy spares his troops but reveals the plan to everyone on the battlefield. Joab prefers sacrificing some of the troops along with Uriah, to make the whole affair appear like an unpreventable and regrettable defeat in battle. He stations Uriah where he knows it is most dangerous, in the path of *anshei chayyil* (אנשי חיל), the mightiest of the enemy warriors. He leaves some of David's own officers at Uriah's side. When Uriah the Hittite falls, so do they (2 Sam. 11:16–17).

Joab is a man who will thrice kill men loyal to or loved by David: Abner, Absalom, and Amasa (2 Sam. 3:27; 2 Sam. 18:14; 2 Sam. 20:10). He does not shrink from killing others along with Uriah. By killing Abner, Joab might have imagined himself as ensuring David's hegemony. Abner had, after all, just changed sides and was long known as Saul's man. Or perhaps, Joab was securing his own position in David's court. Killing Uriah, a man whose soldierly prowess had brought him into David's inner circle, eliminates another competitor. Biblical hegemonic masculinity is the foundation for an honor society in which men engage in ongoing competitions for power.

And so, Joab has only to make sure David gets the right message. His instructions to his messenger are precise. The king may become angry when he hears that many officers died; his envoy should immediately tell the king that his servant, Uriah the Hittite, was among the fallen (2 Sam. 11:19–21). David gets the message and sends his approval back to Joab: "The sword always takes its toll. Press your attack on the city and destroy it! Encourage him!" (11:25). Royal approval has been signaled. Joab is strengthened by what he has done.

Stone writes that "Uriah dies due to a lack of solidarity on the part of his male colleagues, and particularly Joab" (1996, 101). But in fact, Uriah's death is *due to* the solidarity between his male colleagues and Joab who collude with David, not with his Hittite general. Men support the most dominant males, often imagining what it would be like to occupy such dominant positions themselves. And by this time, the fraternities that have demonstrated their loyalty to David have been consolidated. David, unlike his predecessor, has proven he has all it takes to be king: he has slaughtered his enemies and humiliated and feminized them. He has acquired women and sired sons. His men support him in doing more of the same as they work on his behalf. A company of men has been involved in the taking of Bathsheba and in the raping of Bathsheba. A company of men has carried out the king's orders. And, as in the narratives of Tamar and David's *pilagshim*, the taking and raping of women leads to the murder of men.

For the biblical authors, voyeurism and exhibitionism are central not only to Michal's story, but to Bathsheba's. Indeed, there can be little doubt that a male biblical author invites his male audience to become Peeping Toms alongside David and his servant(s), to treat Bathsheba as a tantalizing object.⁵⁸ "By denying her subjectivity, the narrator symbolically rapes Bathsheba," Exum writes, "and by withholding her point of view, he presents an ambiguous portrayal that leaves her vulnerable to the charge of seduction" (2016b, 138). Bathsheba is the victim, as Exum has noted, of a rape by the pen. The narrator permits readers to engage in fantasies about Bathsheba and to simultaneously blame her (158).

Biblical authors valorize men who demonstrate their sexual virility, and David has proven, time and again, his capacity for sexual display. Some scholars have noted with surprise how openly transgressive David's behavior is at the beginning of the narrative. After all, they argue, to commit adultery in the open is an extraordinary and subversive act, given that adultery is the "great sin."⁵⁹ But David's action can be read above all as rape, rather than adultery, and the rape of Bathsheba takes place in a rape culture in which women's bodies are at the disposal of men—especially powerful men. The male biblical author is enjoying David's power; he is partaking in it vicariously, as is his audience. Hegemonic masculinity always involves subordinate men engaging in just such vicarious enjoyment of the sexual power of men who are, as it were, "on top."

In essence, David is hardly less public in his rape of Bathsheba than Absalom is of the rape of David's *pilagshim*. David stands on the roof where Absalom will later commit rape, and there he plans a rape of his own. He ogles Bathsheba, he asks who she is, then sends for her openly; she goes to the palace, and she returns home—none of this is done under the cloak of secrecy. The male biblical audience can experience here the modeling of masculinity at its most blatant. Seeing how power is employed to take a woman and rape a woman is a learning experience for men in a rape culture.

Stone notes that when the deity chastises David, it is after the murder of Uriah, not after the rape of Bathsheba. If all we had was the account of sexual contact, without the treachery and murder that follow, we would likely not see David punished at all (Stone 1996, 97–98).⁶⁰ David is condemned not for his sexual aggression "but rather for transgressing the conventional structures of the male contest for honor and power and disregarding the rights of an honorable man fighting at David's command" (105). Exum, too, argues that David's sin lies in his crimes against Uriah and God, not Bathsheba—in fact: his punishment is "that what he did to another man will be done to him" and this demonstrates "how irrelevant the woman's perspective is" (2016, 147–48).

Yhwh's punishment ramps up the violence; now, he announces, the sword will never depart from the royal house (2 Sam. 12:10). Yhwh will take David's women from him and give them to another man (2 Sam. 12:11). David acted secretly; the deity, however, will inflict his punishment on David publicly (12:12). What David did secretly, however, was the murder, not the rape. When Uriah refused to be David's tool, he had to die. Every step of the planning, every message sent from David to Joab and from Joab to David, every piece of the plot, was performed with subterfuge and guile. It is David's secret machinations that the deity condemns, machinations that resulted in the murder of David's own men.

It is not the rape that the deity denounces. Quite the opposite, in fact. Yhwh moves women's bodies from one man to the other with aplomb and announces his right to do so (2 Sam. 12:8).[61] A deity who punishes a man for murder by delivering his women for another man to rape is not a deity who rejects sexual violence against women. Sexual violence against women poses problems in the Hebrew Bible only when it threatens other men and their control of female bodies. The Israelite deity oversees and even manages a rape culture in which sexual violence is the means for working out male competition for power and authority. Ultimately, Yhwh is in charge.

Conclusion

Michal is surrounded by men from the very outset, all of whom collectively negotiate her marriage to David. Likewise, Bathsheba is surrounded by men from the very outset, all of whom negotiate her rape by David. In both cases we find men at work, doing their king's bidding, facilitating his agenda, and protecting his honor and reputation. David, it turns out, is far more successful than Saul at garnering loyalty, proving himself worthy of the throne, and demonstrating both his military might and sexual potency.

Both stories feature soldiers whose loyalty is at stake and who may die as a result of secret plotting by their own king. Both stories feature foreign enemies that must be subdued and conquered. Both feature generals and advisors whose own grip on power is intimately related to the king they support. Losers, like Paltiel and Uriah, will be humiliated; one trails after Michal in tears, the other is made a cuckold. Both stories demonstrate how the ideal man of the Hebrew Bible exercises his power over women and over the men who serve him, and how kings try to combat the risk of shame and any challenges to their masculine honor. They do so, in significant part, by demonstrating their control over women's bodies, with the overt aiding and abetting of their subordinates.

Exum writes that "male violence begets male violence; it needs no women to give it birth" (2016b, 155). It is, however, obvious that sexual violence against women is one way for men of the Hebrew Bible to negotiate power. Women's bodies are theirs to exploit for the sake of proving who has the right to govern. Biblical authors offer their male audience a treat: stories that confirm their own understanding of what makes a man a man, stories that provide the vicarious pleasure of the ogling, the entrapping, the taking, and the raping of women. Contests over the future of Israel and its governance are tied to sexualized aggression, related to the use of women's bodies, and dependent on the collusion and cooperation of men. Biblical rape culture depends upon them all.

Notes

1 Wives are made available to foreign potentates for their use (Gen. 12), virgins are offered to mobs of men for theirs (Gen. 19:8; Judg. 19:24, 21:20–23). One young woman is gang raped (Judg. 19), and the deity himself engineers the gang rape of Daughter Zion/Israel by her former lovers (Lam. 1:9–10; Ezek. 16:27–41). The list of biblical rapes is longer than the one I offer here.
2 Ken Stone writes: "Sexual activity seems to concern the narrator almost entirely because of *its possible consequences for relationships between men*, and so becomes, within the narrative discourse of the Deuteronomistic History, a primarily homosocial affair. Other male characters are, so to speak, the initial audience of the sexual events that take place. . . . [A]ll of these texts capitalize upon the potential for sexual acts to impact the honor, power, and prestige of the men" (1996, 136–37; italics original).
3 Michal appears six times in the Hebrew Bible (1 Sam. 14, 18, 19, 25 and 2 Sam. 3, 6). In her first appearance, she is listed among Saul's children (1 Sam. 14:49). Some versions of 2 Samuel 21:8–9 also insert Michal's name for Merab's.
4 Ellen van Wolde argues that the author uses Michal's love to place David in a lower hierarchical position, creating a deliberate exception to the rule that love must be expressed from a man toward a woman (22). Nehama Aschkenasy (1998, 36), Cheryl Exum (2016a, 7), Esther Fuchs (2000, 110, 174), Robert Alter (1999, 115 n. 20), and Yaron Peleg (2005, 185) all remark on the singularity of this verse.
5 Jonathan makes his abdication clear by giving David his clothing and armament (1 Sam. 19:3–4).
6 We are later introduced to Rizpah, likely just one of Saul's *pilagshim*. In 2 Samuel 12:8, Yhwh reminds David that he had given him his master's wives. David has had no other master than Saul.
7 Saul makes an untimely sacrifice (1 Sam. 13:9–14), utters a misguided vow forcing his men to hunger while in the midst of battle (1 Sam. 14:24), and does not proscribe, as he was ordered, all Amalek (1 Sam. 15:8–9).
8 The term (חול) appears in Judges 21:20, when the Benjaminites capture young women of Shiloh while they are dancing, taking "dancers" as wives.
9 David later uses this tactic with Uriah, sending him into the thick of battle to die.
10 See also, for example, Stone (1996, 130), Aschkenasy (1998, 36), and Fuchs (2000, 139–40).
11 The deity reproves Samuel for assuming that Eliab, Jesse's impressive eldest, is the man he is to anoint, insisting that he disregard appearance or stature (1 Sam. 16:6–7). Still, looks matter after all. The scene starts with a veritable beauty pageant of Jesse's sons, none of whom fit the bill until David arrives, "ruddy cheeked, bright eyed, and handsome" (16:8–12).
12 Roland Boer points out that this is hardly the first piece of evidence of the deity's admiration for beautiful young men (1999, 29). The deity's first choice for king, Saul, is the tallest and handsomest man among them (1 Sam. 9:2).

13 *El* (אל) is used here.
14 The word commonly deployed for "servant," *eved* (עבד), can refer to a slave, a dependent of some sort, a military subordinate, an official, and adviser, even a minister. See Koehler and Baumgartner 2001, 774–75.
15 Nabal (נבל) means "fool" (Koehler and Baumgartner 2001, 663). Ahinoam is also the name of Saul's wife. The author foreshadows the later transfer of Saul's women to David in 2 Sam. 12:8 (Thiede 2022, 53). See also Jon Levenson and Baruch Halpern (1980, 514) and David Firth (2008, 324).
16 This is in the second of two versions of the story of David's arrival at court. In the first, narrated in 1 Samuel 16, David is meant to soothe Saul, who is afflicted by Yhwh's evil spirit. In 1 Samuel 17, David arrives to provision his brothers and ends by killing Goliath.
17 Taking women demonstrates strength. In Judges 5:30, Sisera's mother imagines him bringing home one or two women for every man (the Hebrew is coarse, referring not to women, but to "wombs"). Ironically, it is the Israelites who have won the battle and likely taken captives. Texts detailing the taking of women as war booty can be found in Numbers 31:17–18, Deuteronomy 20:10–20, and Judges 21:11–12.
18 My choice to transliterate this term is explained in note 12 of the Introduction.
19 Adonijah similarly makes a bid to acquire David's former servant, Abishag. In so doing, he enrages Solomon for his apparent play for the throne and is consequently executed (1 Kings 2:22–25).
20 Again, this is in the second version of the narrative where David is introduced to Saul (1 Sam. 17).
21 Jennings writes: "David displays his body to the one who first desired him for his beauty" (2005, 42), arguing that Yhwh is clearly interested in his chosen men's good looks. Indeed, both Saul and David are noted for their beauty. See 1 Samuel 9:2 and 16:12.
22 J. P. Fokkelman casts David's behavior as an act of religious devotion while noting that Michal understands it as sexual in nature (1990, 199). When women dance, their movements are understood as sexual. When men dance, sexual connotations elude scholarly notice, even if they expose their genitals while dancing and specifically admit that others have been watching, as David does.
23 Observing an act of exposure from a window also occurs in Genesis 26:8, when Abimelech watches Isaac as he engages in fondling his wife. This act leads to Abimelech's humiliation at Isaac and Yhwh's hands (Thiede 2022, 100). As Susanne Scholz points out, the use of the root צחק in Genesis 26 suggests "rape-prone" activity (2021, 90–92). She notes that the root is also used in Genesis 39:14, when Potiphar's wife accuses Joseph of rape (90).
24 The entire house of Israel has been part of the parade (2 Sam. 6:15). The very expression used here, *beit Yisrael* (house of Israel), is like its corollary, *am Yisrael* (people of Israel), an expression that refers to Israelite men. Israel is, by definition, male. Israel is Yhwh's possession, created in order to give Yhwh honor (Isa. 43:7). Given that honor is never applied to women, Israel must, perforce, be male (Clines 2019, 73). The phrase "house of Israel" also refers to men. Female characters, through birthing sons, build up the house of Israel and produce the men who inhabit it (Ruth 4:11).
25 Clines writes that the Song of Songs, too, was produced for the purpose of titillating a male audience with dreams of a fantasy woman unafraid of expressing her sexuality (2009, 94–121).

26 The narrator "uses Michal's protest to eliminate her. . . . She goes to her literary death screaming, as it were" (Exum 2016b, 19). We do not know if David accessed Michal's body after first taking her from Paltiel.
27 Women are never said "to take" a man. See Stone 2015, 175.
28 What happened to Michal when she arrived at David's court goes unstated; what is noted is David's and the deity's rejection of her body *because of her protest*. Just as the Levite's *pilegesh* is punished for leaving Yhwh's priest, so will Michal be punished for disloyalty and disrespect to David. See Thiede 2022, 114–15, 118.
29 In the end, sexual violence will lead to murder, just as it does in the rapes of Tamar and the *pilagshim*.
30 Another biblical example of shaming or humiliating through cutting the beard can be found in Isaiah 7:20. Cynthia Chapman explores how beards demonstrate masculinity in ancient Israel and Assyria (2004, 39). Neo-Assyrian art shows kings with full beards (26). Men are humiliated by being forced to wipe the sandals of their victorious opponents with their beards, and they are depicted being held by their beards (39). Shaving off half of a beard ridicules a man's masculinity (223). Together with the exposure of the men's buttocks, it is clear that sexual humiliation is Hanun's aim.
31 Fokkelman makes this same point, writing that "the theatre of war serves as the background for 11:2–12:25 and is, as such, strictly indispensable to Ch. 11" (1981, 47).
32 Exum notes that David is not alone (2016b, 139). Still, exegetes routinely do not note that at least two men are watching.
33 Marti Steussy asserts that David answers his own question. He points to three consecutive verbs "followed by a rhetorical question without any indication of a change in subject"; in other words, David sent and inquired and said, "isn't this Bathsheba?" (1999, 78).
34 The scholars who have made such a claim are too numerous to list here. Some have accused Bathsheba directly of solicitation. See, for example, George Nicol (1988, 360) and H. W. Hertzberg (1964, 309–10). Alter, in his commentary, intimates it (1999, 251, n. 4). The story has most often been read as a love story: "Visual art, music, and even film have contributed to this view. In paintings of Rembrandt, Cornelis Cornelisz van Haarlem, and Carlo Maratti, the woman is displayed as a nude who offers herself to viewers, as if to reinforce the notion that she is a temptress" (Scholz 2021, 100).
35 Sociologists have analyzed how such modern-day rape myths work. See, for example, Sarah Murnen, Carrie Wright, and Gretchen Kaluzny 2002, *passim*.
36 See also Fokkelman 1981, 53.
37 The text does not specify where Bathsheba took her bath though we do know that it is springtime (2 Sam. 11:1). Tikva Frymer-Kensky argues that cisterns would have been placed on roofs in ancient Israel to collect winter rainwater and that bathing on roofs would have made practical sense (2002, 144). Both archeological and textual records show that ancient Israelites built walls around their rooftops (Deut. 22:8). Clearly, sleeping on rooftops was also not unknown (Josh. 2:8). A biblical audience might have imagined Bathsheba thinking herself sheltered from view by the walls surrounding her. That same audience could picture the Peeping Toms on the palace roof above.
38 Suzie Dunn points out that technology has made stripping a woman without her knowledge easily achievable by, for example, placing a woman's head on a

female body in a sexualized image, hiding cameras and livestreaming intimate images of women's bodies, and inputting a clothed image of a woman to produce a fake nude photo of her. Men are twice as likely to perpetrate image-based abuse than women (2020, 9).

39 In his 1981 film "The History of the World: Part I," Mel Brooks plants his royal face in a woman's cleavage and then announces: "It's good to be the king."
40 "The great sin" (חטאה גדלה) refers to the sin of adultery (e.g., Gen. 20:9). Adultery was likewise considered "the great sin" in Egypt (Rabinowitz 1959, *passim*). Ancient Babylonian law codes prescribe death for adulterers. Mutilation for female offenders is described in Neo-Babylonian marriage contracts (Roth 1988, *passim*). In addition, the "great sin" could result in divine punishment (Westbrook 1990, 566–69).
41 This passage may be compared to Genesis 34:2, in which Shechem sees (ראה), takes (לקח), lays (שכב), and humbles/degrades (ענה) Dinah, and/or to the series of verbs describing the rape of Tamar, in which Amnon seizes (חזק), humbles/degrades (ענה), and lays (שכב) her. For a detailed discussion of the vocabulary in all three scenes, see Andruska 2017, *passim*.
42 Andruska (2017, 104); Koenig (2018, 15). Létourneau also discusses additional variants (2018, 79, n. 22).
43 Originality is a fraught concept where transmission of ancient texts is concerned. "The texts we have in our modern Hebrew Bibles are not some 'first form' with a clear claim to 'originality' . . . our Hebrew Bible is a *version* of biblical writings" (Thiede 2022, 2).
44 My students regularly ask if Bathsheba might have thought she was being brought to the palace because her husband had been killed. Uriah is, after all, one of David's inner circle. Alexander Izuchukwu Abasili makes this suggestion, too (2011, 11).
45 Caroline Blyth also notes that when *shachav* is used to describe sexual encounters, it is generally designating some kind of illicit relation (2010, 49). See, for example, Exodus 22:15; Leviticus 18:22, 20:13; and Deuteronomy 22:22.
46 We see such uses in Genesis 34:2, when Shechem takes Dinah.
47 Exum notes, too, that "the position of the story in the middle of the account of the Ammonite war—but also the aftermath of the encounter suggests force . . ." (2016b, 140).
48 Immediately following the header "What to Do If You Have Been Raped," one writer notes: "Starting from the very beginning, your first instinct might be to take a shower or bath to wash away what has happened to you. This urge is understandable. However, doing this may wash away physical evidence that could be used for prosecution. It is extremely important that before washing yourself or changing, you see a medical professional as soon as possible" (Cornforth 2020). Bathsheba might be seeking to avoid the pregnancy that does ensue. Of course, the Hebrew Bible also legislates washing after sexual acts (Lev. 15:18). Frymer-Kensky believes Bathsheba to be "washing off the impurity that comes from all sexual relations, even licit ones" (2002, 147). Helen Leneman observes that the version of 2 Samuel 11 found at Qumran leaves out the phrase "from her impurity" in verse 4, suggesting that the phrase was added by a later editor due to changing attitudes toward menstruation and impurity (2010, 275). For more on this topic, see Exum (2012, 47), Létourneau (2018, 76), and Koenig (2018, 13).
49 Biblical authors frown on women leaving their homes (e.g., Gen. 34, Judg. 10). The messenger is likely male.

50 Again, the term used here, *am* (עם), refers to the men of Israel, not some generic "people." See note 24.
51 See also Stefan Schorch 2000, 194–96.
52 Michael Flood discusses the role of sex talk that involves urging another man to have sex with a woman (2008, 346).
53 Stone's *Practicing Safer Texts: Food, Sex, and Bible in Queer Perspective* explores the connections between food and sex in detail.
54 Stone notes that Uriah's question makes clear that he is aware of what David intends and regards sleeping with Bathsheba as a breach of honor and a betrayal of his fellow soldiers suffering at the front (1996, 100). One must also consider that Uriah's refusal to play David's game may also demonstrate resistance to being used.
55 Flood details how heterosexual sex becomes a channel for homosocial bonding. The sex may be mutually experienced as a fantasy, as a performance for the men involved, or as shared sexual acts (2008, 351–52).
56 Gale Yee notes that Uriah can eat and drink in David's presence, and even be made drunk by him, but refuse to eat and drink with his wife (1988, 246). Away from the front, male-male homosociality is permitted. Being fooled is not.
57 David signing Uriah's death warrant echoes how Saul sends his messengers to guard and arrest David (1 Sam. 19:11). Both kings attempt to do away with the men who lead their troops in war; both direct others to do the dirty work.
58 The male biblical author invites his male audience to become Peeping Toms alongside David and his servant(s). Deryn Guest resists the binary thinking of the male biblical author: "I do not stand as David, but alongside David, vying for Bathsheba's attention, challenging his values, his performance of masculinity, offering Bathsheba a different option, and representing the presence of female homoeroticism" (2008, 249).
59 Regina Schwartz writes: "Adultery clearly threatens the identity of Israel" (1991, 48). Frymer-Kensky notes the gravity of adultery as a capital offense (149) but observes that "the king can act and the people will accept" (2002, 147).
60 Stone uses the phrase "sexual contact" to describe what happens between David and Bathsheba (1996, 98).
61 Sharing women among men actively increases the deity's own reputation and honor as we see in the "sister-wife" stories of Genesis 12, 20, and 26 (Thiede 2022, 86–109).

Bibliography

Abasili, Alexander Izuchukwu. "Was It Rape? The David and Bathsheba Pericope Re-Examined." *Vetus Testamentum* 61, no. 1 (2011): 1–15.

Alter, Robert. *The David Story: A Translation with Commentary of 1 and 2 Samuel.* New York: Norton, 1999.

Andruska, Jennifer. "Rape in the Syntax of 2 Samuel 11:4." *Zeitschrift für die alttestamentliche Wissenschaft* 129, no. 1 (2017): 103–9. doi:10.1515/zaw-2017-0007.

Aschkenasy, Nehama. *Woman at the Window: Biblical Tales of Oppression and Escape.* Detroit: Wayne State University Press, 1998.

Blyth, Caroline. *The Narrative of Rape in Genesis 34: Interpreting Dinah's Silence.* Oxford: Oxford University Press, 2010.

Boer, Roland. *Knockin' on Heaven's Door: The Bible and Popular Culture.* Biblical Limits. New York: Routledge, 1999.

Chapman, Cynthia R. *The Gendered Language of Warfare in the Israelite-Assyrian Encounter.* Winona Lake, IN: Eisenbrauns, 2004.

Clines, David J.A. *Interested Parties: The Ideology of Writers and Readers of the Hebrew Bible.* Sheffield: Sheffield Phoenix Press, 2009.

Clines, David J.A. "The Most High Male: Divine Masculinity in the Bible." In *Hebrew Masculinities Anew*, edited by Ovidiu Creangă, 61–82. Hebrew Bible Monographs 79. Sheffield: Sheffield Phoenix Press, 2019.

Cornforth, Tracee. "Surviving and Healing After Rape." *Verywellhealth*. Accessed November 18, 2020. www.verywellhealth.com/rape-healing-and-survival-35 20427.

Dunn, Suzie. "Forms of TFGBV." In *Technology-facilitated Gender-Based Violence: An Overview*, edited by Suzie Dunn, 5–16. Centre for International Governance Innovation, January 1, 2020. Accessed June 12, 2021. www.jstor.org/stable/resrep27513.10.

Exum, J. Cheryl. *Plotted, Shot, and Painted: Cultural Representations of Biblical Women*, 2nd ed. Sheffield: Sheffield Academic Press, 2012.

Exum, J. Cheryl. "Desire, Love, and Romance in the Hebrew Bible." *Oxford Research Encyclopedia of Religion* (June 9, 2016a). Accessed October 23, 2021. www.oxfordre.com/religion/view/10.1093/acrefore/9780199340378.001.0001/acrefore-9780199340378-e-54. doi:10.1093/acrefore/9780199340378.013.54.

Exum, J. Cheryl. *Fragmented Women: Feminist (Sub)versions of Biblical Narratives*, 2nd ed. London: Bloomsbury T&T Clark, 2016b.

Firth, David G. "David and Uriah (With an Occasional Appearance by Uriah's Wife): Reading and Re-Reading 2 Samuel 11." *Old Testament Essays* 21, no. 2 (2008): 310–28.

Flood, Michael. "Men, Sex, and Homosociality: How Bonds Between Men Shape Their Sexual Relations with Women." *Men and Masculinities* 10, no. 3 (2008): 339–59. doi:10.1177/1097184X06287761.

Fokkelman, J.P. *Narrative Art and Poetry in the Books of Samuel, vol. 1, King David.* Assen, The Netherlands: Van Gorcum, 1981.

Fokkelman, J.P. *Narrative Art and Poetry in the Books of Samuel: A Full Interpretation Based on Stylistic and Structural Analyses, vol. 3, Throne and City.* Assen, The Netherlands: Van Gorcum, 1990.

Frymer-Kensky, Tikva. *Reading the Women of the Bible: A New Interpretation of Their Stories.* New York: Schocken, 2002.

Fuchs, Esther. *Sexual Politics in the Biblical Narrative: Reading the Hebrew Bible as a Woman.* London: Bloomsbury, 2000.

Guest, Deryn. "Looking Lesbian at the Bathing Bathsheba." *Biblical Interpretation* 16, no. 3 (2008): 227–62. doi:10.1163/156851508X247611.

Hertzberg, H.W. *I and II Samuel: A Commentary.* Translated by J.S. Bowden. The Old Testament Library. Philadelphia: Westminster, 1964.

Jennings, Theodore W. *Jacob's Wound: Homoerotic Narrative in the Literature of Ancient Israel*. Biblical Studies/Old Testament. New York: T&T Clark, Continuum, 2005.

Koehler, Ludwig, and Walter Baumgartner. *The Hebrew and Aramaic Lexicon of the Old Testament*, vol. 2. Leiden: Brill, 2001.

Koenig, Sara M. "Make War Not Love: The Limits of David's Hegemonic Masculinity in 2 Samuel 10–12." *Biblical Interpretations* 23 (2015): 489–517. doi:10.1163/15685152-02345p02.

Koenig, Sara M. *Bathsheba Survives*. Columbia, SC: University of South Carolina Press, 2018. doi:10.2307/j.ctv6mtf4t.

Leneman, Helen. *Love, Lust, and Lunacy: The Stories of Saul and David in Music*. Bible in the Modern World. Sheffield: Sheffield Phoenix Press, 2010.

Létourneau, Anne. "Beauty, Bath and Beyond: Framing Bathsheba as a Royal Fantasy in 2 Sam 11, 1–5." *Scandinavian Journal of the Old Testament* 32, no. 1 (2018): 72–91. doi:10.1080/09018328.2017.1376523.

Levenson, Jon D., and Baruch Halpern. "The Political Import of David's Marriages." *Journal of Biblical Literature* 99, no. 4 (December 1980): 507–17. doi:10.2307/3265190.

Levine, Baruch. "Religion in the Heroic Spirit: Themes in the Book of Judges." In *Thus Says the Lord: Essays on the Former and Latter Prophets in Honor of Robert R. Wilson*, edited by Claudia V. Camp and Andrew Mein, 27–42. Library of Hebrew Bible/Old Testament Studies 502. New York and London: T&T Clark, 2009.

Murnen, Sarah K., Carrie Wright, and Gretchen Kaluzny. "If 'Boys Will Be Boys,' Then Girls Will Be Victims? A Meta-Analytic Review of the Research that Relates Masculine Ideology to Sexual Aggression." *Sex Roles* 46, no. 11 (June 2002): 359–75. doi:10.1023/A:1020488928736.

Nicol, George G. "Bathsheba, a Clever Woman?" *The Expository Times* 99, no. 12 (March 1, 1988): 360–63. doi:10.1177/001452468809901203.

Peleg, Yaron. "Love at First Sight? David, Jonathan, and the Biblical Politics of Gender." *Journal for the Study of the Old Testament* 30, no. 2 (December 1, 2005): 171–89. doi:10.1177/0309089205060606.

Rabinowitz, Jacob J. "The 'Great Sin' in Ancient Egyptian Marriage Contracts." *Journal of Near Eastern Studies* 18, no. 1 (January 1959): 73. www.jstor.org/stable/543942.

Roth, Martha T. "'She Will Die by the Iron Dagger': Adultery and Neo-Babylonian Marriage." *Journal of the Economic and Social History of the Orient* 31, no. 2 (1988): 186–206. www.jstor.org/stable/3632097.

Scholz, Susanne. *Sacred Witness: Rape in the Hebrew Bible*. Minneapolis: Fortress Press, 2021.

Schorch, Stefan. *Euphemismen in der Hebräischen Bibel*. Orientalia Biblica et Christiana 12. Wiesbaden: Otto Harrassowitz, 2000.

Schwartz, Regina M. "Adultery in the House of David: The Metanarrative of Biblical Scholarship and the Narratives of the Bible." *Semeia* 54 (1991): 35–55.

Steussy, Marti J. *David: Biblical Portraits of Power*. Studies on Personalities of the Old Testament. Columbia, SC: University of South Carolina Press, 1999.

Stone, Ken. *Sex, Honor and Power in the Deuteronomistic History*. Journal for the Study of the Old Testament, Supplement Series, 234. Sheffield: Sheffield Academic Press, 1996.

Stone, Ken. *Practicing Safer Texts: Food, Sex, and Bible in Queer Perspective*. London and New York: T&T Clark International, 2005.

Stone, Ken. "Marriage and Sexual Relations in the World of the Hebrew Bible." In *The Oxford Handbook of Theology, Sexuality, and Gender*, edited by Adrian Thatcher, 176–77. Oxford: Oxford University Press, 2015. doi:10.1093/oxfordhb/9780199664153.013.020.

Thiede, Barbara. *Male Friendship, Homosociality, and Women of the Hebrew Bible: Malignant Fraternities*. Routledge Studies in the Biblical World 5. London and New York: Routledge, 2022. doi:10.4324/9780429326226.

van Wolde, Ellen J. "Sentiments as Culturally Constructed Emotions: Anger and Love in the Hebrew Bible." *Biblical Interpretation* 16 (2008): 1–24. doi:10.1163/156851508X247602.

Westbrook, Raymond. "Adultery in Ancient Near Eastern Law." *Revue Biblique* 97, no. 4 (October 1990): 542–80. www.jstor.org/stable/i40170770.

Yee, Gale A. "'Fraught With Background': Literary Ambiguity in II Samuel 11." *Interpretation: A Journal of Bible and Theology* 42, no. 3 (July 1, 1988): 240–53. doi:10.1177/002096438804200303.

3 The Once and the Future King
Saul, David, and the Practice of Sexual Violence

Introduction: What Makes a King?

The king of the ancient Near East is a warrior among warriors, a man who feminizes as well as kills his enemies. Enemies are ridiculed, cursed, shamed, and mutilated. They are dubbed passive and weak, and described as women. The Assyrians demand divine aid in making their enemy "like a woman" (Chapman 2004, 48). Jeremiah taunts the warriors of Babylon for refusing to fight: "They sit in the strongholds, Their might is dried up, They become women" (Jer. 51:30). David curses Joab, declaring that his house will never be without men who take up the spindle and act like women (2 Sam. 3:29). Insult gives way to injury. The enemy's masculinity is denied him. Defeated kings and soldiers are stripped of their clothing and armor, impaled, and beheaded (1 Sam. 31:8–9; 2 Sam. 23:10).[1]

The Hebrew Bible presents us with an honor culture. In such cultures a man who has been dishonored "surrenders his own masculine identity and becomes a woman who is victimized and penetrated" (Gilmore 1987, 11). To shame a man not only divests him of prestige, it suggests a loss of male social identity, of masculinity itself (ibid.). The defeated warrior is, metaphorically, a woman who has been raped (Niditch 2008, 6). The savagery of ancient texts is hardly metaphorical, however. The man who does not merely die by the sword, but who has his head cut off, his extremities amputated, or his foreskin sliced from his penis, is the victim of sexualized violence.[2] Just as women can be sexually assaulted without penile penetration, so can men.[3] In the Hebrew Bible, sexual assault sometimes takes place when men are already dead.

Sexual violence against men is as key to the David story as is sexual violence against women. The rape of men propels David's rise, demonstrating both his might and his right to the throne. In the Hebrew Bible, a man who would be king is a man who commits sexual violence; such a man has the qualifications and the resumé the Israelites and their deity value. One's

DOI: 10.4324/9781003014911-4

king, like one's god, should be a warrior who can and will slay with impunity and humiliate every enemy before him. The ideal man—and the ideal king—is David, a most efficient rapist and killer.[4]

Yet the first human ruler of Israel was not David, but Saul. Scholars have spent decades comparing Saul and David, explaining why the former fails as a king and the latter is chosen to replace him. Saul is indecisive, unsure of himself, his connection to Yhwh mediated through Samuel. "Ambivalence and oscillation are the hallmarks of the story of Saul," writes Robert Alter (1999, xix).[5] There is another reason Saul fails, however: he is not capable of the level of violence David deploys. He tries, of course, but his attempts go awry, often in ways that invite ridicule.

From the moment David steps onto the scene, the biblical narrative is awash in sex and sexual violence. It is David who shows what it means to be good at being a man. As an ideal male, *the* ideal male of the Hebrew Bible in fact,[6] he ruthlessly humiliates and exterminates his enemies, acquires women (sometimes from other men), and sires a goodly number of sons. Taking and raping women is a specialty of David's house, not Saul's. What the biblical audience (and the modern reader) discover in the David narratives is unsettling: the man who is best at sexual violence is the most powerful in all Israel and most worthy of the kingship.[7] He will practice sexual assault against men and against women. The rape of men is as key to his success as is the rape of women.[8]

Biblical rape culture underpins every move men make in their competitions for power. And here, too, in the raping of men, we will find the rapist supported, aided, and abetted by a company, even an army, of men. The king who does not have his men behind him is not a successful rapist and does not deserve their loyalty. David, not Saul, will be the king to remember. Through utilizing sexualized violence on a vast scale, he will earn the admiration and loyalty of all Israel, attaining power and status. Saul, in comparison, is a mere amateur.

Saul: The Man Who Could Not Be King

When we first meet Saul, he seems bursting with kingly potential. His credentials include both singular good looks and an impressive lineage. Saul's father, Kish, is a wealthy and important member of the tribe of Benjamin (1 Sam. 9:1). Saul, in turn, stands out in a crowd. No man of Israel was better looking than Saul (ואין איש מבני ישראל טוב ממנו);[9] he is "head and shoulders" (משכמו ומעלה גבה מכל העם) above all other Israelites (1 Sam. 9:2). But Saul is not the paragon of determination, conviction, or power we might expect from the first man to be crowned king of Israel.

From the outset of his story, Saul proves to be dependent on others for advice, counsel, and direction. He is chosen by a resentful and jealous deity who is unhappily giving in to his people's desire for a king to be set in his place (1 Sam. 8:7). Once chosen, Saul is directed by Yhwh's prophet Samuel, who puts him to task and then appears to set him up for failure. Saul never achieves the support of the deity who singled him out—not once does Yhwh speak directly to Saul as he does to so many of the men of his choice.[10] Saul also never manages to collect a company of men whose loyalty is without question. In his performance of masculinity, he is, from the start, inadequate.

We first meet Saul working as a kind of farm hand, out hunting wayward donkeys. He is accompanied by a servant, who must guide and counsel his master.[11] As Alter notes (1999, 47 n. 5), Saul's first words are a question: should the two men should give up the search and return home (1 Sam. 9:6)? It is the servant who suggests Saul consult a man of God (the prophet Samuel); it is the servant who knows where the man of God is to be found; and it is, astonishingly, the servant who produces coin for acquiring the intel they need. Saul does not come prepared; his servant does. Saul does not take charge; his servant does.

Yhwh chose Saul for Israel's first king, but in one episode after another, the erstwhile farmer proves hesitant and unsure of himself. Moreover, Saul is often caught between Yhwh and Samuel. When Samuel summons the Israelites to Yhwh at Mizpah for Saul's crowning, the audience is treated to a burlesque scene. Samuel uses lots to divine Yhwh's will. The tribes of Israel are brought forth until Benjamin is indicated, then Saul's clan, then Saul himself. But Saul is nowhere to be found (1 Sam. 10:17–21). Yhwh must reveal the truth: Saul is hiding among the baggage, curling up his tall and powerful man's body like a child (10:22). Saul is forced from his hiding place. "There is none like him among all the people," Samuel proclaims (10:24). And the people shout: "Long live the king!" But Saul's embarrassment, his reluctance, even his fear, remain memorable. This is a king who is so terrified to take on the role that he hides from those who would hand it to him.

Saul is a doubtful candidate. Yhwh influences the men who accompany him to Gibeah (1 Sam. 10:26); these are men "whose hearts God had touched" (החיל אשר נגע אלהים בלבם). Yhwh feels the need to ensure their loyalty to Saul and, in so doing, help Saul gain the popularity a new king should possess. Other men, however, recall Saul cowering among the baggage and question Saul's ability to save them (10:27). The narrator calls these men "worthless fellows" (בני בליעל), hinting that the audience can anticipate that Saul will be more capable than the "bad" men give him credit for. But only up to a point.[12]

The Once and the Future King 77

The ideal man of the Bible does not hide when called to power. He does not hesitate to take charge. He is rhetorically adept. He bonds with other men. He possesses honor and power and incessantly strives for more. Saul's rule will demonstrate his dependence on other men. David will prove his ability to dominate them. Saul's first battle scene is stellar proof: this man can only be king because others have manipulated him.

Pressed into the role of king, Saul faces his first military challenge almost immediately. Just after Saul returns home, Nahash the Ammonite besieges Jabesh-gilead. The men of the town seek to avoid wholesale slaughter by offering up their bodies in servitude. Nahash agrees, but on one condition: each man of the town will have his right eye gouged out (1 Sam. 11:1–2). "I will make this a humiliation for all Israel," the Ammonite ruler declares (11:2). The word the biblical author deploys, *herpah* (חרפה), is associated with shame and has undeniable sexual connotations. In 2 Samuel 13:13, Tamar uses this same term when she asks Amnon, "where will I carry my shame (חרפתי)?" Prophetic texts, too, use *herpah* to show how the deity inflicts shame. The enemy Yhwh dishonors, whether it be Babylon, Chaldea, or Jerusalem, is feminized (Isa. 47:3; Ezek. 16:57). Nahash is doing what an effective king does to his enemies: he is threatening to inflict a humiliation that is sexual in nature and feminizing too—to debase a man is to make him a woman.[13]

Yhwh responds with a penetrative move, ensuring that Saul, his hesitant retainer, will succeed at the bloody business of fighting. He turns Saul into a berserker by rushing divine power into Saul's all-too human body (1 Sam. 11:6).[14] The deity's spirit, the *ruach Elohim* (רוח אלהים), is forced into Saul, making him capable of performing "manhood acts."[15] Saul's anger blazes up. He takes a yoke of oxen, cuts them up, and sends their pieces throughout Israel with a warning: "Thus shall be done to the cattle of anyone who does not follow Saul and Samuel into battle" (11:6–7). Yhwh's *ruach Elohim* makes the man.

Saul is flooded with a divine power, one that is intimately tied to the human performance of masculinity (Murphy 2015, 176). But despite the *ruach Elohim*, Saul's actions could have been even more extreme. When a leader needs to gather his men for battle, he sends animal or human parts out to each tribe or constituent group. The parts are brought to the gathering site. When all the severed parts are brought together, the troops are ready for war (Liverani 2004, 162). Saul uses oxen. In Judges 19 and 20, we read how one of Yhwh's priests cuts up a woman's body in order to muster the troops.[16] And we learn from Judges 11 that the sacrifice of human bodies— here, a virgin daughter—facilitates victory and ensures the deity's commitment to the cause (Judg. 11:34–39).[17]

Saul's first battle is successful. The Ammonites are defeated. But not all are killed: survivors scatter after the battle (1 Sam. 11:11). It also took

Yhwh's intervention to make Saul act the man in the first place. The *ruach Elohim* grants courage, drives battles, elects, and dismisses leaders—it is, as Murphy notes, "an integral part of what it means to be a man (or to be unmanned) in the narratives of Judges and 1–2 Samuel" (2015, 177). Nevertheless, Saul will not be on divine steroids for long.

On his own, Saul is frequently hesitant, timid, and anxious—all of which may explain why his men do not fully trust him. After he defeats Nahash, it is Saul's son Jonathan, not Saul, who strikes down the Philistine prefect (1 Sam. 13:3). Men gather to Saul at Gilgal to pursue the war against the Philistines but must delay; sacrificing to Yhwh is necessary to ensure divine favor. Samuel has demanded that Saul wait until he arrives to supervise the ritual. But Samuel fails to show up at his own appointed time (13:8). One cannot help but wonder why Samuel is dilly-dallying; surely, he must be well aware that the troops will get restive without clearly demonstrated divine approval. Indeed, the men begin to scatter. Saul panics, performing the sacrifice himself (13:9). For this, he is roundly censured. Samuel announces that because Saul did not obey the prophet, Yhwh will now abandon Saul and seek out a new man, a man after his own heart (13:13–14).

Saul has no company of men to defend him. Far from it. He cannot keep his men from abandoning the field, though he tries. His efforts to hold his men together are rejected by Samuel and, it would seem, by the Israelite deity. Saul has barely become Yhwh's and Samuel's man before the two decide he is unworthy of their support. Saul's tendency to panic, to overreact, and to fail at the task of being a man becomes ever more apparent. When Jonathan makes a sortie against the Philistines with only his arms bearer and Yhwh to support him, Saul authors his own misfortune and makes lasting triumph impossible. He insists that his men refrain from eating until he can follow up on Jonathan's foray and complete his revenge on the enemy. But Saul's uncalled-for oath leaves his men hungry and weak (1 Sam. 14:24), unable to succeed in supporting their king's plan. Saul gives up the chase and the Philistines escape to fight another day (14:46).

Jonathan unknowingly violates his father's foolish vow. Saul attempts to act the man by sentencing his son to death. Those who violate the king's vow can have no excuse, after all, even if they are prince and heir to the throne. Saul is thwarted (and undermined!), however, by his own soldiers, who insist he leave Jonathan unharmed. Saul blames those selfsame soldiers when Samuel calls him to account in the next chapter for failing to carry out *ḥerem* (חרם) against the Amalekites (1 Sam. 15:20–21).[18] Later, when Saul demands that his own guards slaughter the priests of Nob, not one of his own men lifts a hand (1 Sam. 22:17). Instead, an Edomite must do Saul's dirty work (22:18–19). Saul is *not* a ruthless or even decisive ruler of men, and his men know it. His relationships with the men he commands are not merely weak, they are broken.

In neo-Assyrian textual traditions, fearful and defeated rulers are feminized (Chapman 2004, 72). After Samuel dies, Saul is so uncertain of his aims that he first forbids any recourse to necromancers, only to ask his courtiers to find *him* one to consult (1 Sam. 28:3, 7). Yhwh has refused to respond to the king's entreaties; desperate measures are in order (28:6). For Saul, there is no one left but the ghost of Samuel, the prophet who once left him in the lurch and then denounced him (13:8, 13–14).

It is a desperate man who seeks the necromancer. Saul disguises himself and tries to hide his identity—this king cannot even play the king. The necromancer is not fooled. She accuses Saul of laying a trap for her, first by banning her work, then by demanding she divine for him (1 Sam. 28:9). Saul assures her of her safety and asks her to bring Samuel up from the dead (28:10–11). Upon arrival, the prophet sounds the death knell (again) of Saul's rule: Yhwh has torn the kingdom from him and handed it to David (28:17–18). Further, his defeat will bring Saul's death and that of his sons. Terrified, Saul falls to his knees. His downfall is a literal one. And like all military defeats, it is emasculating: Saul is prostrate on the ground, weak and powerless. He must depend on a woman to feed him, to strengthen him, to get him back on his feet. The irony and the insult are obvious. A feminized Saul is manned up—by a woman.

We might recall that Barak insists on having Deborah's support before going to battle (Judg. 4:8). She agrees, but a devastating pronouncement accompanies her assent: there will be consequences for his womanish behavior. He will reap no glory in the coming victory. The prophetess and judge announces that Yhwh will deliver Sisera into the hands of a woman instead (4:9). Deficient warriors are shown up by women and even led by women. In the worst possible cases, they may be killed by them (Judg. 4:21; 5:26–27; 9:53).

Saul's last battle is a final, absolute humiliation. The king himself makes crystal clear what he fears. Philistine arrows have drawn blood. Saul is seriously wounded, but refuses to grant his enemy the final thrust. "Draw your sword," he tells his armor bearer, "and run me through, so that the uncircumcised may not run me through and make sport of me" (1 Sam. 31:4). Translations suggest the Philistines will insult Saul ("make sport of"), but the Hebrew is more graphic. The verse includes the hitpa'el form of *alal* (עלל) coupled with the prefix *bet* (ב), a combination that indicates sexual violence. The phrasing used here, *v'hital'lu bi* (והתעללו בי), is found in Judges 19:25, when the Levite's *pilegesh* is taken and gang raped by a mob of men. The men raped her and, as most translations render the phrase, "abused her" (ויתעללו בה) all night long.[19]

Saul has reason to fear sexualized violence at the hands of the enemy. He is already pierced and penetrated, wounded by arrows. The Philistines may decide to run him through more than once, effectively gang raping him with their weapons as the men of Gilead gang raped the *pilegesh* with their members. In the ancient Near East men are supposed to penetrate and kill their enemies and, afterwards, perform additional acts of sexual violence on their enemies' corpses. Saul knows he may be raped not just while alive, but after his death.

Saul's arms bearer refuses to accede to Saul's request (1 Sam. 31:4). Saul has only one way to mitigate the sexualized violence he can expect to endure. He dies by his own sword, successfully penetrating . . . himself (31:4). And what he might have feared and could not control, nevertheless comes to pass: When the Philistines find his corpse, they strip him, decapitate him, impale him, and display his body (31:9–10).

Saul has his moments of magnanimity, humility, generosity, and even kindness. He responds humbly to Samuel when they first meet, insisting that he comes from the smallest of Israel's tribes and hardly deserves the attention or the honor the prophet offers him (1 Sam. 9:21). Though some Israelites question his election, Saul refuses to put to death those who doubted him (11:12–13). Samuel reproves Saul for conducting a sacrifice Samuel should perform, but Saul's decision to make an offering to Yhwh after Samuel failed to appear as promised was as an attempt to steady his men for battle (13:8–9).

Still, Saul is most often depicted as a failed king. Not once do we see Saul using his spear in battle. Instead, we see Saul hurling his spear at David (1 Sam. 18:10–11, 19:9–10), and then Jonathan (20:33). He misses every time. In fact, he has so little control over his weapon that David can take it from him while he sleeps (26:12). The sexual connotations are obvious: Saul is unable to dominate because he is unable to penetrate.[20] He is not a king among men—he is not, perhaps, even good at being a man among men. In the end, the narrative will prove many times over all the ways in which Saul is unsuited to kingship. He will be driven mad, left naked, and exposed, humiliated by the deity who regrets making him king in the first place (15:11). Saul is depicted, and not infrequently, as a caricature of a king.

What can David possibly learn from such a man? Saul should be modeling masculinity, and that includes powerful displays of persuasive skill, physical power, and military prowess. He should be showing his own men what a king must possess: strength, courage, and virility. Going out to battle is his task; when the Israelites ask for a king, they list exactly this as their primary need (1 Sam. 8:20). He should taunt his enemies, humiliate them, and violate them. Instead, Saul becomes, if unwillingly, ever more dependent on other men to play the man for him. When he dies, the enemy does to him what he was supposed to do to them. He is stripped of his armor, decapitated, his body impaled and displayed (31:9–10).

Saul is not an entirely unsuccessful warrior. He has killed his thousands (1 Sam. 18:7). But he falls short. When David arrives at his court, Saul's inability to control even his own men, much less defeat and humiliate his enemies, becomes increasingly apparent to the biblical audience. His example, where masculinity is concerned, mainly shows his shortcomings. He has not outmanned all other men or mastered the art of inflicting sexual violence on others. It is David who will demonstrate how to be the best at such things, and it is David who will gather a company of men to collude in and support the abundant sexual violence he commits.

David at Saul's Court

Saul is rendered inadequate in both versions of David's arrival at court.[21] In the first, David arrives to help heal the king of divinely induced madness. Yhwh, who once had filled Saul with his divine spirit (1 Sam. 10:10), has stripped him of it. It is now David who possesses Yhwh's powerful *ruach*. In what appears a downright vindictive move, Yhwh plagues Saul with an evil spirit (16:14), a *ruach ra'ah* (רוח רעה). What Yhwh giveth, he taketh away, and purposefully. The mad king is now succored by none other than the man destined to be the next king, David. Yhwh, who created Saul's terror and his trouble, now arranges the (temporary) cure. Saul's courtiers reassure him: David will be able to heal the king with a soft voice and a lyre. They praise David's many attributes. David is a skilled musician, a stalwart fellow, a warrior, a persuasive speaker, and good-looking to boot (16:18).[22]

Immediately upon arrival, David is the object of Saul's appreciative gaze; the king appears to fall in love at first sight.[23] The young boy who won the beauty pageant at his father's home (1 Sam. 16:12) finds his good looks appreciated at Saul's court.[24] Saul, the biblical author tells us, loves David greatly (ויאהבהו מאד), and he does all that he can to keep the young man close by (16:22). He sends word to Jesse, David's father, that David will stay at court. He makes sure David will stay right at his side, too, as his arms bearer.[25] David is pleasant to look at and finds favor in Saul's eyes (16:22).[26] The young musician takes on a wifely role with his new master, consoling, succoring, and healing Saul when he is troubled (Thiede 2022, 39–40).

In the second of the two narratives depicting David's introduction to the royal court, the audience is likewise treated to a vulnerable king. Saul has not gone out to battle the enemy who taunts him and his men. By refusing to fight Goliath, Saul effectively violates the terms of his contract: a king's job is to lead the charge (1 Sam. 8:20). There are no accounts of Saul taunting the Philistines. There are no accounts, either, of him mutilating his enemies. Rather, though Saul kills some of his enemies and harries others, he also lets some get away.[27] It is David who goes forth to fight Goliath, the Philistine hulk who has struck terror into the heart of every last Israelite man but for the young lad who lives among the sheep. That lad will present masculinity *par excellence*, taunting the enemy, feminizing him, and humiliating him. David will make evident the kind of sexualized violence that rulers must master.

David appears in this story as a mere boy among men, the youngest of eight brothers, most of whom are still too young to fight with Saul.[28] Jesse, David's father, deploys his youngest son as a courier for the eldest three, who are fighting alongside Saul. He sends David to the battlefield to bring supplies, including bread, parched corn, and cheese, to his brothers and to the captain of their division (1 Sam. 17:17–18). The king is unable to fully provision his troops—another sign of Saul's failings. Just as David arrives with the goods, the Israelites and the Philistines draw up their battle lines. David unloads and heads straight to the front. Goliath steps forward and the men of Israel flee, terrified (17:20–24). In this moment, it is neither King Saul nor his men who can face the Philistines. The Israelite warriors are all turned into women.

The soldiers talk amongst themselves. The one who kills the monstrous enemy before them will be richly repaid, they say, and not just with monetary rewards but with the king's own daughter. David does not waste any time in making sure he has heard correctly: "What will be done for the man who kills that Philistine and removes the disgrace from Israel?" he asks (1 Sam. 17:26). David uses the word *herpah* here (מה יעשה לאיש אשר יכה את הפלשתי הלז והסיר חרפה מעל ישראל), a word with obvious sexual implications, as we have seen. Goliath's very existence shames and feminizes the men (and their king). David immediately makes sure, therefore, to display his own manly loyalty to the man of all men, Yhwh. "Who is that uncircumcised Philistine," he asks, "that he dares defy the ranks of the living God?" (17:26). The story is told again, and though his eldest brother Eliab chastises him for his arrogance and presumption, David is uncowed. He goes from one set of troops to the next, asking each time for information about the promised reward.[29] David has an opportunity to make a man of himself on every front—and in clear contradistinction to the Israelite soldiers and their king. If he succeeds, he shows he is no longer the "boy" he is labeled by both Goliath and King Saul (17: 33, 42). If he gets a woman and a princess into the bargain, so much the better.

Everyone underestimates the young man who preens before them. When Saul protests that David is just a boy and cannot possibly fight Goliath, David boasts that he has won in hand-to-hand combat against bears and lions who threatened his father's sheep (1 Sam. 17:33–34). First, he would free the sheep from the mouth of whichever ferocious animal had dared

The Once and the Future King 83

to seize it. "And if it attacked me," he adds, "I would seize it by the beard and strike it down and kill it" (17:35). For an English reader, the word "beard" (זָקָן) seems misplaced. But it is a telling choice. As we saw in Chapter 2, neo-Assyrian representations show kings in battle with developed musculature, an erect stance, an unflinching gaze, and full beards (Chapman 2004, 26). Kings who surrender to others wipe the victorious ruler's sandals with their beards, and prisoners are depicted being held by the beard just before their heads are cut off (39). "What was going on in these instances was a humiliation of the foreign king's claim to masculine honor," Chapman writes (ibid.). And indeed, when David's own messengers are humiliated by Hanun, the Ammonite, by having their beards half shaven and their buttocks exposed, David tells his men to remain in Jericho until their beards are grown again. Only then, when they are men again, may they return (2 Sam. 10:5).[30] David makes it clear: a young boy who can hold the most ferocious of animals by the beard—the very symbol of *über*-masculinity, royal authority, and power—is a fit opponent for the giant Goliath.

The biblical male must be a "fighting male" (Clines 2009, 216). Men win honor, prestige, and status when they boast victory in war. David not only proves he is a real man, he parades the fact that he knows what kings do. Defeating a fearsome enemy in single combat provides a grand performance of masculinity. Who should be king of Israel? Not Saul, obviously, who is now the sort of warrior Jeremiah taunts for staying at home and becoming a woman (Jer. 51:30). And so, David goes out to meet Goliath. Saul tries to clothe him in his own battle gear before he leaves, hoping to substitute his armor for his body and demonstrate his prowess by proxy. But David cannot walk in the tall king's armor. Doing so would send the wrong signal. Had he fought dressed in Saul's armor he might have owed the king some credit for the defeat of Israel's enemy.[31] Instead, he wisely takes it off, picks up five smooth stones and goes to battle carrying his sling in his hand (1 Sam. 17:39–40).

The battle scene is replete with sexual associations, and violent ones at that. As Stephen Wilson notes, the author combines a verb for strength, *ḥazak* (חזק), together with the preposition *min* (מן)—a combination often translated as "overpowered" (1 Sam. 17:50). Such a usage is, however, elsewhere connected to sexual violence against women. David overpowers the Philistine (ויחזק דוד מן הפלשתי) just as his own son and heir, Amnon, will overpower and rape his half-sister Tamar in 2 Samuel 13:14 (ויחזק ממנה). The author's choice of words "may serve as rhetorical propaganda depicting Goliath as a feminized sexual victim of the newly minted man, David" (Wilson 2015, 101). Sexual associations, Wilson adds, permeate the actual method of execution. David approaches Goliath with his " 'stick in his hand' and a pouch full of stones" (101–2). On its own, the death of the Philistine feminizes him. But David kills him with weapons that stand for his own genitalia, as Wilson suggests.

Goliath's death is humiliating and feminizing in the extreme. After killing him, David immediately pulls Goliath's own sword from its sheath and cuts off his head, completing the degradation of Goliath's body (1 Sam. 17:51).[32] David uses Goliath's own weapon, which stands for his own member, to take his head from his body. It is shameful.[33] And though Goliath's end appears to make Saul's rule secure, the death of the giant foreshadows Saul's own degrading death; he, too, dies by his own sword and he, too, is decapitated by the enemy (31:4, 9).

By this time, the biblical audience knows that Saul is not the proper man for the throne. He does not succeed as a rapist of men, despite his many military victories. Where David will crush and conquer his opponents, Saul will only harry them, ensuring in the long run that they will return to avenge themselves. It will not be the tallest of the Israelites, the first to be called king, who faces Goliath; it will be David, who cannot walk in Saul's clothes and, perhaps, should not try, either. Saul was afraid to become king and is afraid to act like one. David, in contrast, shows how a king should behave, by killing the enemy in a way that is explicitly sexually charged.

Once Goliath has been done away with, David is within his rights to expect that Saul pony up on the promise to give his daughter to the young warrior. Indeed, Saul will do just that, but not as a reward for David's triumph. Instead, Saul will try using his daughter against David. The king is afraid. David has, in short order, managed not only to defeat Israel's premier enemy, but also to make a conquest of practically every man and woman in Israel. Saul's son, Jonathan, Saul's troops, Saul's courtiers, the women of every single Israelite town, and Saul's daughter, Michal, admire, praise, and love their new hero, who is beautiful, fierce, and sexually aggressive (1 Sam. 18:5–7, 20).

Explosive sexual tension is endemic to this narrative. Once Goliath is killed and mutilated, David is brought before Saul. We know from the first version of David's arrival at court that Saul is homoerotically attached to his arms bearer. Now, we will discover how Saul's son, Jonathan, experiences *his* first sight of David. Once again, David makes a conquest: "Jonathan's soul became bound up with the soul of David; Jonathan loved him as himself" (1 Sam. 18:1). Saul saw David and loved him at first sight (16:21). Jonathan does the same. David's own emotions are immaterial. In 1 and 2 Samuel, a man good at being a man elicits passion and sexual attention. He is admired for his beauty; men may openly love him for it.

Saul reacts to Jonathan's infatuation by making his own claim on David clear. Saul "takes" (לקח) David and refuses to let him go back to his own father's house (1 Sam. 18:2). This is exactly how a woman is made a wife: she is "taken." Her sexuality is transferred from father to husband when she leaves her paternal home for her husband's house.[34] Saul and his son are now competitors for David's attention. Jonathan ups the ante by handing over his robe and tunic to his newly beloved, as well as his sword, bow, and belt (1 Sam. 18:4). What once was next to Jonathan's skin now graces David's.[35] Few Israelites own swords, and according to the biblical author, Saul and Jonathan are the only ones who carry one into battle (13:22). Jonathan's sword clearly symbolizes his exceptional status. There is yet another layer of homoerotic attachment being revealed here: Jonathan has handed David the most potent and powerful symbol of his manhood. And handing over his princely clothing to David has political import, too. Once, Jonathan could show up Saul through his own courage and bravery (14:1–15). Saul's troops loved him and defended the prince—even against his own father, the king. But now Jonathan is unmanned, willingly spending the rest of his life supporting and loving David—just as an ideal wife would do.[36]

After making a conquest of both king and prince, David proceeds to do the same with the rest of Israel, men and women alike. The Israelite troops, in the course of a single chapter, become David's men. He does not have a mere company behind him, but an entire army. Saul makes him his general, and David's every success earns him admiration (1 Sam. 18:5). When the young warrior returns successfully from battle he is feted, too, by the women of Israel who come out from their towns to dance before him (18:6). The text claims they are coming out to greet and congratulate Saul. But when the dancing women begin to sing, they make clear whom they celebrate: "Saul has slain his thousands," they sing, "David, his tens of thousands!" (18:7). David has displaced the king by doing Saul's job, killing and unmanning Israel's greatest enemy, Goliath, and defeating the Philistine army. He has acquired the attention and affection of all Israel. The man who is meant to rule has conquered men and women alike.

Saul still imagines that he can control David, and even do away with him. One way to do exactly that is through the use of a woman's body. But Saul's attempt to use Michal's love for David backfires spectacularly. David does not die gathering up the bride price Saul has demanded, he doubles it, returning from battle with the foreskins of not one hundred but two hundred Philistines. Saul's new leader of men effectively castrates the enemy Saul cannot himself conquer (1 Sam. 18:27). Again, the enemy is unmanned twice over: first, by death, then by emasculation. Davis is already expert at humiliating, degrading, and feminizing his enemies.

Saul kills his thousands, but we know of no killing that was succeeded by the mutilation and emasculation of his enemy. Such is not true of the future king of Israel; David mutilates and emasculates his enemies with dedication. Those who battle alongside David witness the evidence; David shows who is truly fit to be king. Again: the death of a man on the battlefield is comparable, for biblical authors, to his rape. But where Saul kills some and lets others flee, David will desecrate corpses, in effect raping his enemies twice (1 Sam. 17:50–51; 18:27). He is the better rapist not just of women, but of men too.

The king is unmanned. Saul grows yet more afraid of his rival—and fear is womanly. Saul makes desperate attempts to demonstrate who is man of the house by calling on the men he supposedly commands. He goes both to his courtiers and Jonathan, urging them to kill David (1 Sam. 19:1). But Saul has not succeeded in building the partnerships, coalitions, and friendships he needs. His soldiers had refused to kill Saul's son Jonathan, and his courtiers do not agree to kill his son-in-law either. Yhwh, too, has long since abandoned Saul, and Samuel, who announced the demise of his house, is nowhere near. Even Jonathan refuses to do his bidding, instead playing mediator. He warns David of Saul's anger and reminds Saul of David's courageous conquest of Goliath (19:5). Saul is convinced—temporarily—to leave David in peace, but Yhwh intervenes, again sending his evil spirit into Saul while David plays before him. Saul, who holds his spear (and thus, symbolically, his manhood) in his hand, tries to pin David to the wall with his weapon, but fails. Saul is not capable of the kind of sexualized violence against another man that is expected of him as king; he is not nearly the rapist David has already become.

Michal makes it possible for David to escape Saul's murderous wrath, but Saul persists in imagining he will be able to do away with his son-in-law. Once he discovers David's whereabouts, he sends out messengers to seize him. Yhwh intercedes again, making fools of the king's men by sending them into a prophetic frenzy (1 Sam. 19:20). Saul sends more men, but the pattern is repeated (19:21). Saul's company of men are as ineffectual as their leader: Saul is inadequate, and so are the men he manages to retain.[37]

Yhwh adds insult to injury, inflicting the same humiliation on Saul when he decides to go after David himself. Saul's madness is driven to extremes in a public setting. In a divinely-induced frenzy, Saul strips off his clothes and lies naked a day and a night (1 Sam. 19:24). Nakedness is shameful, and Saul's fall from grace is public, pathetic, and absurd.[38] The author makes the people's reaction proverbial: "That is why people say: 'Is Saul too among the prophets?'" (19:24).

This is not the first time Saul has been driven to a prophetic frenzy. Nor is it the first time such a question has been asked. A prophetic ecstasy comes upon Saul as part of his election in 1 Samuel 10. Then, too, the people ask: "What's happened to the son of Kish? Is Saul too among the prophets?" (10:11). In this first episode the people wonder about Saul with a kind of amazement. The second episode is different. Stripping off his kingly clothes to lie naked, elicits a deprecatory response from the Israelites, as it must. Saul's fall from grace is public and unforgettable. The biblical author makes sure of that. As he writes, "that is why" the people say what they do about Israel's first king.

Saul has become a laughingstock. He will try to reassert his authority; once again, he will reach for the very symbol of his manhood, his spear, as his weapon. This time, he will threaten his own heir. But before trying to execute his own son, Saul unleashes a tirade, one which publicly demeans, humiliates, and exposes his own wife.[39] The entire scene is fraught, a family affair. Saul's violent language is provoked by the loss of David, a beloved retainer who had served in a subordinate, even wifely role to him (Thiede 2022, 39–40). David is now the dominant man in a homoerotic relationship with Jonathan, and it is Saul's son who plays the loyal wife to the young general. Saul has lost both David and his son; now he fears Jonathan will assist David in taking his wife, his son and heir, and the throne.

David has just found a way to dismiss the king. In an emotional scene, he and Jonathan discuss Saul's murderous anger. Shocked by David's insistence that Jonathan kill him if he can be proven guilty of any crime against Saul, Jonathan responds with equal melodrama: Yhwh should strike *him* dead if he does not tell David the truth about the king's intentions (1 Sam. 20:13). Then Jonathan invokes Yhwh, praying that he be with David as he once was with Saul (20:13). The prince renews his covenant with David, swearing, once again, his love (20:17).[40]

David, in turn, concocts a story for Jonathan to transmit to the king. Jonathan is to tell his father that David asked the prince's permission to visit his own father's home in Bethlehem for an annual sacrifice (1 Sam. 20:6).[41] Jonathan does as asked (20:28). Perhaps he doesn't think through the consequences. For Saul and his attendant court, it must appear that Jonathan has usurped a kingly prerogative: namely, the right to sanction and approve David's movements. Not unsurprisingly, when Saul is confronted with the layered insults in the tale, he understands that David has left him for good. In front of his men, at a public feast, he shouts:

> You son of a perverse, rebellious woman. I know that you side with the son of Jesse—to your shame, and to the shame of your mother's nakedness. For as long as the son of Jesse lives on earth, neither you nor your kingship will be secure.
>
> (1 Sam. 20:30–31)

Saul demands that Jonathan bring David to him to be executed. David, Saul states unequivocally, is now a dead man (20:31). Saul betrays his weakness publicly in a desperate effort to protect his rule and his authority from a virile young challenger. He exposes his wife, Ahinoam, otherwise wholly hidden from view, by evoking her naked body for all the men present. Saul's courtiers share the queen's body with their king, if only in their imaginations.

The wording of this passage has been extensively explored.[42] Its significance as an indicator of rape culture has not. The language found here is symptomatic, however—clearly revealing a culture in which women's bodies become the site for exercising male authority and male sexual violence. Ahinoam is never named. In addition, Saul's angry tirade foreshadows what will happen in David's own reign; the rape in this text anticipates rapes to come.

The king condemns his son for his alliance with David, charging him with betrayal. When Saul accuses Jonathan of handing over all Israel and Judah to David, he effectively implies that every female body the king controls will be handed over too. To take the throne is to take the king's women. Jonathan has, from Saul's perspective, made it possible for David to acquire Saul's wife (Seebass 1977, 53).[43] It may be clever foreshadowing on the author's part, for later, when David is king, Nathan reminds him: "Thus said the LORD, the God of Israel: 'It was I who anointed you king over Israel and it was I who rescued you from the hand of Saul. I gave your master's house *and possession of your master's wives*; and I gave you the House of Israel and Judah'" (2 Sam. 12:7–8, italics mine). Nathan adds a warning, declaring that David, too, will live to see his own women taken from him (2 Sam. 12:11).[44]

But Saul is not merely lambasting his son for abandoning his mother to David. Saul's language is the language of rape culture, which routinely describes women in the crudest possible ways and insults men by calling them into women. He calls Jonathan the son of a "perverse, rebellious woman" (בן נעות המרדות), using a term for Jonathan's mother that means "twisted" or "bent" (עוה). The root for the word "rebellious" (מרד) has sexual connotations: it can evoke the meaning "wayward" (Alter 1999, 128 n. 30) and is elsewhere used to describe Israel's faithlessness (Ezek. 2:3; Josh. 22:16, 18–19; Dan. 9:9). Saul bitterly suggests that his son's loyalty to David is offered up to his own shame and to the shame of his mother's nakedness (לבשתך ולבשת ערות אמך). Alter observes that the language "has virtually the force of 'your mother's cunt'" (1999, 128 n. 30). Two terms used here, "shame" (בשת) and "nakedness" (ערוה), both refer, in the Hebrew Bible, to genitalia.[45] Saul calls his wife, in effect, an adulteress, even a whore, and Jonathan is shamed and insulted along with her.[46]

Then and now, a man condemns and degrades another man by comparing him to a woman.[47] Jonathan is named wayward and twisted along with his mother. But it is Ahinoam's body which becomes the vehicle for the prince's public humiliation. Jonathan's shame is, in Saul's words, the same as his mother's genitalia. He is made a woman alongside her, and both are made faithless, bent, and perverse—both are whores, in the king's eyes. We should recognize the trope. Biblical texts regularly turn masculine Israel into a feminized object, one whom the deity shames and degrades in word and deed (Isa. 47:3; Jer. 13:20–27; Hos. 2:5; Ezek. 16:27–41, 23:17–21; Nah. 3:5–6; Lam. 1:9–10). In a rape culture, Yhwh can call for the public humiliation, even rape, of Israel; his kings can do the same to their wives.

Saul's language is largely analyzed for what it reveals about his fury against David and his rage toward Jonathan.[48] Yet, what the biblical author presents here is an ancient version of the sexual assaults we regularly witness in our own time, assaults that rely on using language and images to debase, vilify, and silence women.[49] Sexual harassment includes making derogatory and debasing remarks about women's bodies. Men share such comments with one another, cementing homosocial bonds at women's expense. In today's wired world, sharing and commenting on image-based sexual abuse is likewise a way for men to bond with one another, to reinforce toxic gender norms, and to demonstrate structures of male domination (Dunn 10).

Saul essentially calls his queen the biblical equivalent of a "slut." He refers to her genitalia in the crudest possible terms. He labels her faithless, evoking the adulteress and the whore. He does all this before his courtiers, at a public celebration, during a feast. No man present at Saul's court protests the king's diatribe. Instead, they collude. Saul's son is publicly feminized, and Ahinoam pays the price for her son's humiliation. In evoking her genitalia, Saul and the biblical author expose her nakedness to everyone. Such texts, written for a male audience, might have provided the sexual charge a deepfake porn video can offer men of our own time.[50] The readers, too, become party to Ahinoam's utter debasement. She is a victim of sexual violence through words and images. Such forms of assault are found in the Hebrew Bible every time the deity threatens to expose Israel to sexual violence. The biblical author depicts a king who is following Yhwh's lead. It is the one rape Saul is still capable of carrying out, one his men clearly do not find in the least unsettling. Saul's own wife is his easy target. Wives often are.[51]

The postscript to the scene is yet another rape attempt. Saul picks up his spear, intending to throw it at his son and heir, Jonathan. But Saul is inept when it comes to inflicting sexualized violence on men. A humiliated, feminized Jonathan leaves Saul's court to return to his beloved David and to invoke, again, their shared oaths. He is demeaned, but alive (1 Sam. 20:33–34, 41–42). The narrator has made his case. Saul is incapable of committing the kind of sexual violence the king of Israel should.

David: The Man Who Will Be King

David, even in exile, nevertheless manages to continue demonstrating his own fitness for royal power. First, he needs food for his men and weaponry for war. Ahimelech, priest at Nob, offers him both. David's men receive consecrated bread, though he must first assure the priest that neither he nor his men have had sexual congress with women (1 Sam. 21:5–6). One of Saul's men is present at the scene, the Edomite Doeg. He witnesses David asking Ahimelech if he has a spear or sword available for the young general's use (22:9). He does, and offers up Goliath's sword. David is now big enough to hold the weapon of a giant. The sexual overtones are obvious (22:10).

David's brothers join him, together with every man who is experiencing the stress of war (1 Sam. 22:1–2). In the meantime, Saul pursues David, stopping at Nob and questioning Ahimelech. Saul accuses the priest of colluding with David and orders his men to kill all the priests. But no servant of the king will comply with such orders; Saul may be king, but he is no ruler of men (22:17). Finally, Saul turns to the foreigner, Doeg the Edomite, to do his dirty work. And Doeg proves he is the man Saul will never be: he kills everyone—eighty-five priests, men, women, children, and infants. Not even the livestock are safe from his sword (22:18–19).

David continues to battle the Philistines, doing the work of the king and protecting the Israelites. He shows who should *really* stand at their head. Yhwh is with him and offers guidance at every step (1 Sam. 23:1–13). And so it goes: David continues to fulfill kingly responsibilities while the actual king neglects the enemy without, preoccupied with the enemy he fears within.

Despite the exigencies of constant battle and a struggle to keep himself and his men alive, David acquires one woman after another. Saul offers Michal to another man, but David has already found himself two new wives. Once again, the biblical text makes Saul into a laughingstock. The first woman David takes is named Ahinoam, like Saul's own queen. The author suggests that David's new wife is a different woman by designating her origin—she is named as "Ahinoam of Jezreel" (1 Sam. 25:43). Nevertheless, for the biblical audience, the allusion is obvious. Once, the king publicly evoked the image of David taking *his* woman, the queen. Now, the audience may justifiably, even if only momentarily, imagine David doing just that.[52] The same chapter that details the wiving of Ahinoam of Jezreel features a second woman, Abigail. When her husband Nabal dies of fear of retribution from the young warrior, she neatly becomes an addition to David's collection (25:39–42). David takes women from men whose masculinity is debatable and eclipsed.[53]

David's virility is a topic; Saul's is not. Saul is thrice made king before the biblical author names his children (1 Sam. 14:49). His wife Ahinoam is mentioned as an afterthought (14:50). David's acquisition of wives and relationships with women, on the other hand, are thematized. Michal's attraction to David and her acquisition take up nearly half of 1 Samuel 18; moreover, her aid in David's escape is critical to the chapter that follows. 1 Samuel 25 reveals how Abigail practically engineers her own transfer from Nabal, the fool, to David, defender of Israel. And prior to the deaths of Saul and Jonathan, David nearly loses both Ahinoam and Abigail to the Amalekites, who capture them in a raid (30:2–3). Backed by Yhwh, David catches the enemy off guard, slaughters them all, and secures both wives and spoil (30:16–18). Triumphantly, the biblical author announces that the house of David "kept growing stronger, while the House of Saul grew weaker" (2 Sam. 3:1). Victory on the battlefield and in the bed make a man a good candidate for the throne: the verse following the trumpeting of David's strength notes that he has now acquired six different sons by six different wives, one of whom is a king's daughter (3:2–5). Does David even need Saul's women when he has already procured his own harem?

It would seem so. It is no accident that the narrator first informs the audience that David has taken Ahinoam of Jezreel and Abigail and immediately follows this by noting that Saul has married off his youngest daughter a second time, to a man by the name of Paltiel (1 Sam. 25:44). Perhaps, Michal heard that David had married two other women and sees no reason to remain fettered to him. Possibly, Saul intends to strip the young upstart of at least some of the legitimacy he had gained through his marriage to the princess. If David is no longer the son-in-law of the king, his claim to the throne is less potent—he no longer has the king's daughter at his side. Retaking Michal, however, appears largely to serve David's clean-up operations against the remnants of Saul's house. David arranges her return and humiliates her brother Ish-bosheth in one fell swoop (2 Sam. 3:14).

By this time, David has managed to acquire the loyalty of even Saul's men. Abner becomes a turncoat and, as we have seen, his change of loyalties is brought about over access to the body of Saul's concubine, Rizpah. Ish-bosheth's former captains, Rechab and Baanah, betray their king, killing Ish-bosheth in his sleep and decapitating him (2 Sam. 4: 5–7). They bring the severed head straight to David (4:8), who proves himself the greater man by executing *them* and ordering their hands and feet cut off and displayed (4:12). Burying Ish-bosheth's head is David's last act before becoming king. Immediately thereafter the tribes of Israel come to Hebron to offer their full support (5:1). And what do they say? "Long before now, when Saul was king over us, it was you who led Israel in war; and the LORD said to you: You shall shepherd My people Israel; you shall be ruler of Israel" (5:2). Even when Saul was king, he wasn't. David was meant for the job all along. He is crowned king (5:3).

Conclusion

David's journey to the throne provides an object lesson in what constitutes a true ruler: a fearless and ruthless warrior, one who commits sexual violence against men and women alike. He receives collusion, loyalty, admiration, and adoration from the men who follow him. It is not a mere company who backs his every move, but all Israel. Saul is Yhwh's failed experiment, a man who cannot be made after the deity's (violent) heart after all. David can. Along his path, he kills men, women, and children—on Yhwh's behalf.

Saul is hesitant, indecisive, inadequate. He can never truly be sure of his rule over other men—from the start, the Israelites suspect he is not man enough for the job. He fails at creating alliances, the friendships, and networks to support any sexual violence he might commit. David, on the other hand, benefits from just such networks because he is the epitome of the ideal male and, as such, receives the validation and the collaboration of other men.

Saul's men know that he is weak, that his connections with other men are desperate and needy. They are right. Saul cannot be king because he does not succeed at the things that matter most: humiliating, feminizing, and sexually assaulting Israel's enemies and regulating the bodies of the women he should, by rights, control. When he tries to use Michal as his tool to control David, David ends up the winner—escaping Saul's killing rage with her help. When he demeans his own queen, Ahinoam, by evoking her naked body before his guests and labeling her, in biblical terms, no less than a "slut," the author implies that it is David who will own (an) Ahinoam instead of Saul. When Saul raises his spear, throwing it at David (or Jonathan), casting the very symbol of his manhood in an act of murderous violence, the spear misses its mark; Saul cannot penetrate.

David, on the other hand, can. Still in his boyhood, he kills Goliath with weapons that evoke his virility. He cuts off the giant's head, feminizing him and, in effect, raping him a second time. The same goes for the two hundred Philistines David kills and then symbolically castrates, cutting their foreskins from their bodies to present to the king. David knows how to commit all kinds of sexual assault. As David first arrives at court, becomes Saul's general, escapes to build his own army, and eventually takes the throne, his story brims with sex and sexual violence of some kind at every step.

1 and 2 Samuel reveal that the man who commits sexual violence on the greatest scale with the most ease is the man who deserves to be king. He is a man who takes and rapes women; he is a man who sexually assaults men—once, by killing them, and a second time by defacing their corpses. Once king, David and his sons will excel at raping women in the way most familiar to the modern reader. David will himself rape, he will help his first son to rape, and he will practically invite his third son to commit a mass rape.

What we have noted about David's capacity for sexual violence needs to be understood, however, in its entirety. The rape of men is part and parcel of what makes David an ideal man. Biblical rape culture offers the reader a world in which sexual violence of every possible kind is sanctioned and valorized, especially when the king or his deity commits it. David demonstrates how well he can kill and feminize his enemies. Supporting him will be not merely a company of men, but all the men of Israel. Yhwh, too.

Notes

1 See also Chapman 2004, 27.
2 Sexual allusions accompany the removal of limbs and heads (Lemos 2006, *passim*; Lazarewicz-Wyrzykowska 2010, 180–81).
3 Assuming penile penetration proves that a man has been assaulted is a rape myth (Greenough 2020, 9).
4 Clines notes that as the model for the ideal man Yhwh is an unparalleled warrior and killer. Of the seven key words in Hebrew for "killing," Yhwh is the subject of all of them. The same is true for vocabulary around destroying (2019, 69–70).
5 One relatively recent treatment of Saul's masculinity can be found in Măcelaru 2017, *passim*.
6 Clines jump-started the discussion of the ideal man using David as his prototype. David is a powerful warrior, a persuasive speaker, a man who bonds with men while remaining womanless (unless in a procreative or sexual relationship), musical, and good-looking (2009, 216–27).
7 One male is more powerful than Israel's king: Yhwh, who models the sexual violence that his favorites commit. Yhwh labels Israel a harlot and a whore, exposing her to humiliation, gang rape, and stoning by a mob (Hosea 2:12–13; Ezek. 16:15–43; 23:1–49). Biblical writers reveal toxic attitudes to women who are sex workers.
8 Solomon continues his legacy. When Adonijah challenges Solomon's control by making a claim for Abishag, Adonijah is executed. Solomon ensures others do the killing (1 Kings 2:25). He acts similarly in executing Joab (1 Kings 2:34). Solomon proves his virility by acquiring a harem of a thousand women (1 Kings 11:3) and, like David, he humiliates his enemies by enslaving them (1 Kings 9:21).
9 Ralph Hawkins argues that the word *tov* (בוט) implies moral goodness as well as beauty (2012, 357–59).

10 Cheryl Exum notes: "Indeed, Yhwh never addresses Saul directly in the narrative, but speaks to him only through Samuel, or, as in 1 Samuel 14, through the sacred lots" (1992, 23).
11 The servant may not be younger than Saul. Theodore Jennings imagines Saul and his servant as a "relational paradigm" in which a hero is accompanied by a younger male companion (2005, 4). Such relationships are explored in Halperin (1990, 75–87) and Hammond and Jablow (1987, 241–58). The term used here, *na'ar* (נער), suggests a young man of up to twenty years of age, unmarried and without children, but can also be used for servants, courtiers, priestly functionaries, and soldiers (Wilson 2015, 52).
12 Some strands of the Saul-and-David narrative valorize Saul as a humble and courageous man. The dominant view, however, presents David as the superior king and argues that Yhwh has reasons for rejecting Saul.
13 Eyes may symbolize a man's testicles; the effect of eye-gouging is castration (Lazarewicz-Wyrzykowska 2010, 180–81).
14 The term *tzalakh* (צלח) is used in 1 Sam. 10:10 and in 11:6 to describe how the spirit comes to Saul. It connotes mighty and violent force (Levine 2009, 35–36).
15 Douglas Schrock and Michael Schwalbe define "manhood acts" as behaviors "claiming privilege, eliciting deference, and resisting exploitation" (2009, 281).
16 See Judges 19:29–30. "The use of a human corpse as the support for a message is not exceptional in Israel and the ancient Near East in general" (Liverani 2004, 164–66).
17 Yhwh does not intervene to stop Jephthah from sacrificing his daughter, as he does in Genesis 22 to prevent Abraham from sacrificing Isaac.
18 In this case, *herem* (חרם) refers to the total extermination of the enemy and all he owns.
19 The third-person feminine "her" is used here, of course. The same phrase (והתעללו בי) occurs in Jeremiah 38:19 as in 1 Samuel 31:4. Translators use sexually graphic words like "abuse" or "rape" about the *pilegesh* but offer different language ("make sport of") when the same Hebrew expression is used about the abuse of male characters.
20 The spear "symbolizes royal power" (Polak 2011, 59). Roland Boer notes that "the Hebrew word *nkh*, to strike or pierce is another verb that signals penetration . . . images of penetration are part of the male relationships, but here it is signally fruitless, for Saul seems to be shooting blanks at both son and lover" (1999, 30). The spear represents Saul's manhood, a manhood that can be taken from him.
21 The first version begins in 1 Samuel 16, just after Yhwh withdraws his support from Saul and directs Samuel to find the king's replacement. The second narrative is found in 1 Samuel 17 and centers on Goliath and his cause of death.
22 Clines relies on this very verse to define the ideal man (2009, 216).
23 Though appearance is rarely described in the Hebrew Bible, it is key to both 1 and 2 Samuel. David's beauty is described in both versions of his arrival at court. Saul, Eliab, David, Absalom, Adonijah, Abigail, Tamar, Bathsheba, and Abishag are all called beautiful. As Michael Avioz notes, Samuel is the only Deuteronomist work that treats beauty as a subject (2009, 359).
24 Eliab is so attractive that Samuel assumes he is Yhwh's choice (1 Sam. 16:6). Yhwh chooses David, who is "ruddy-cheeked, bright-eyed, and handsome" (16:12).

The Once and the Future King 95

25 Here, Saul negotiates a kind of marriage to David (Thiede 2022, 39–40).
26 The phrasing here indicates sexual attraction (cf. Ruth 2:2, 10, 13; Esther 5:2, 7:3). When a woman loses favor in her husband's eyes (לֹא תִמְצָא חֵן בְּעֵינָיו), she may be divorced (Deut. 24:1).
27 As already noted, some Ammonites survive Saul's attack in 1 Samuel 11. While Saul succeeds in subduing his enemies (1 Sam. 14:47–48), they are not vanquished. David, on the other hand, *will* subdue them (2 Sam. 8:1) *and* enslave the peoples he defeats (2 Sam. 8:2–6; 13–14).
28 Eliab, the first born; Abinadab; and Shammah are among Saul's forces (1 Sam. 17:13).
29 David is clever. If many men claim that Saul has made such promises, Saul will be under pressure to reward whoever defeats Goliath (Thiede 2022, 41).
30 I discuss this material in chapter 2 for its effect on David. Chapman's discussion of beards as signifiers of masculinity is located in n. 30.
31 I am indebted to Johanna Stiebert for this point.
32 Wilson observes that David is never again called a *na'ar* after he defeats Goliath (2015, 100).
33 The decapitation of Holofernes shames his entire army and even the house of Nebuchadnezzar (Lemos 2006, 236). Other examples of shaming through decapitation are found in 2 Samuel 4:8, 2 Samuel 20:21–22, and in 2 Kings 10:6–11.
34 Stone 2015, 176–77.
35 Clothes given from one man to another, Rhiannon Graybill writes, serve as "an alibi for male touch" (2019, 34).
36 Others note Jonathan's wifely role (e.g., Harding 2013, 221; Ackerman 2005, 223). Yaron Peleg suggests that Jonathan is made wifely vis-à-vis David to reveal his unfitness for the kingship (2005, 189). I argue that David becomes a man by rejecting his wifely role to Saul to become first husband and ruler to Jonathan, then to all the women of Israel (2022, 42–58).
37 As we saw in Chapter 2, Saul's messengers act fearfully and even comically, running back and forth from Michal to Saul (1 Sam. 19:11–16).
38 To lose one's clothes is to lose dignity and honor (Măcelaru 2017, 59). Ora Prouser notes that "in a sense, God, too, was involved in disrobing Saul" (1996, 32). Nakedness is a source of shame beginning with the second Creation story (Gen. 3:7). Uncovering the wrong kind of nakedness is taboo (Lev. 18:6–18).
39 Saul has been humiliated by Jonathan. He now humiliates his wife (and Jonathan's mother) in public. A man shamed by another male turns on a woman *he* can shame. In *Wuthering Heights*, Edgar abuses his wife Catherine after Heathcliff insults Edgar. When Edgar insults Heathcliff, the latter attacks his wife Isabella (who is also Edgar's sister). In a complex version of this dynamic, Stamp Paid imagines murdering his wife, Vashti, for her affair with her master's son in Toni Morrison's *Beloved*. Thanks to Clayton Tarr and Maya Socolovsky for these examples.
40 Some suggest Jonathan is asking David to swear his loyalty to the prince. Alter's translation suggests Jonathan is swearing his love to David (1999, 126).
41 David is signaling that he will never again play the role of Saul's wife; he has returned to his father's house without his erstwhile husband's permission (Thiede 2022, 49–51). The Levite's *pilegesh* does the same (Judg. 19:2). Of course, David is not actually at Jesse's house, but in hiding.

42 See, for example, Harding (2013, 204–12), Jennings (2005, 27), Ackerman (2005, 187–88), and Schroer and Staubli (1996, 28).
43 Assyrian royal inscriptions indicate that a defeated king's wife and concubines are spoil (Chapman 2004, 35).
44 As we have seen, Absalom does exactly that, taking and raping his father's concubines before the men of Israel (2 Sam. 16:22).
45 The two terms are used together in Micah 1:11.
46 Johanna Stiebert observes: "Saul has levelled the charge at Jonathan that, in dividing loyalty between his father and David, he has acted disloyally and shamefully—much as though he had committed incest with his own mother" (2016, 136).
47 Men insulting men accuse each other of being "like a girl" or "pussies."
48 Shroer and Staubli treat Saul's tirade as proof of his shame around Jonathan's homosexuality (1996, 19). Peleg suggests that Saul is criticizing Jonathan for being a "mama's boy" (2005, 185). Such observations are worthwhile. Still, we should go beyond exploring male-male relationships to address the rape culture governing them. Harding does, however, remark on Horst Seebass' argument (2013, 209–12).
49 Sexual violence and the growth of technology-facilitated gender-based violence against women is a global phenomenon. Intimate images are taken, manufactured, or disseminated without consent. Images taken with consent are published without it (e.g., "revenge porn"). Innocuous images are sexualized by placing one woman's face on another woman's naked body. Such images are shared in the "manosphere," a collection of men's groups including incels (involuntary celibate men), alt-right groups, and so-called men's rights activist (MRA) groups. Ninety-six percent of sexual deepfakes are of women. Victims have been threatened with actual attack; some have committed suicide. Men plan the making of rape videos for publication. Sexual violence is racialized: women of color are at more risk than white women (Dunn *passim*).
50 Rana Ayyub went to the police with the fakeporn video made of her. She found them watching it themselves: www.huffingtonpost.co.uk/entry/deepfake-porn_uk_5bf2c126e4b0f32bd58ba316 (updated November 21, 2018).
51 See note 39. Laws criminalizing rape in marriage are recent and do not exist everywhere. Marital immunity for rape was abolished in England in 1991 and in 1993 in the United States.
52 Orally, this could be cleverly delivered: "And David took Ahinoam," [pause] "of Jezreel." Jon D. Levenson and Baruch Halpern suggest the women are one and the same (*passim*). The appellation "of Jezreel" suggests they are not. Allusion, though, makes the point. David has access to all the women of Israel, including, by proxy, the king's consort.
53 Nabal (נבל) means "fool."

Bibliography

Ackerman, Susan. *When Heroes Love: The Ambiguity of Eros in the Stories of Gilgamesh and David*. New York: Columbia University Press, 2005.

Alter, Robert. *The David Story: A Translation with Commentary of 1 and 2 Samuel*. New York: Norton, 1999.

Avioz, Michael. "The Motif of Beauty in the Books of Samuel and Kings." *Vetus Testamentum* 59 (2009): 341–59. doi:10.1163/156853309X445025.

Boer, Roland. *Knockin' on Heaven's Door: The Bible and Popular Culture*. Biblical Limits. New York: Routledge, 1999.

Chapman, Cynthia R. *The Gendered Language of Warfare in the Israelite-Assyrian Encounter*. Winona Lake, IN: Eisenbrauns, 2004.

Clines, David J.A. *Interested Parties: The Ideology of Writers and Readers of the Hebrew Bible*. Sheffield: Sheffield Phoenix Press, 2009.

Clines, David J.A. "The Most High Male: Divine Masculinity in the Bible." In *Hebrew Masculinities Anew*, edited by Ovidiu Creangă, 61–82. Hebrew Bible Monographs 79. Sheffield: Sheffield Phoenix Press, 2019.

Dunn, Suzie. *Technology-Facilitated Gender-Based Violence: An Overview*. Report. Centre for International Governance Innovation, 2020, 5–16. Accessed June 12, 2021. www.jstor.org/stable/resrep27513.10.

Exum, J. Cheryl. *Tragedy and Biblical Narrative*. Cambridge: Cambridge University Press, 1992.

Gilmore, David D. "Introduction: The Shame of Dishonor." In *Honor and Shame and the Unity of the Mediterranean*, edited by David D. Gilmore, 2–21. American Anthropological Association 22. Washington: American Anthropological Association, 1987.

Graybill, Rhiannon. "Elisha's Body and the Queer Touch of Prophecy." *Biblical Theology Bulletin* 49, no. 1 (February 2019): 32–40. doi:10.1177/0146107918818042.

Greenough, Chris. *The Bible and Sexual Violence Against Men*. Rape Culture, Religion and the Bible. London and New York: Routledge, 2020.

Halperin, David M. *One Hundred Years of Homosexuality: And Other Essays on Greek Love*. New York: Routledge, 1990.

Hammond, Dorothy, and Alta Jablow. "Gilgamesh and the Sundance Kid: The Myth of Male Friendship." In *The Making of Masculinities: The New Men's Studies*, edited by Harry Brod, 241–58. New York: Routledge, 1987. doi:10.4324/9781315738505-15.

Harding, James E. *The Love of David and Jonathan: Ideology, Text, Reception*. Sheffield: Equinox, 2013.

Hawkins, Ralph. "The First Glimpse of Saul and His Subsequent Transformation." *Bulletin for Biblical Research* 22, no. 3 (2012): 353–62.

Jennings, Theodore W. *Jacob's Wound: Homoerotic Narrative in the Literature of Ancient Israel*. Biblical Studies/Old Testament. New York: T&T Clark, Continuum, 2005.

Lazarewicz-Wyrzykowska, Ela. "Samson: Masculinity Lost (and Regained?)." In *Men and Masculinity in the Hebrew Bible and Beyond*, edited by Ovidiu Creangă, 172–87. Hebrew Bible Monographs 62. Sheffield: Sheffield Phoenix Press, 2010.

Lemos, T.M. "Shame and Mutilation of Enemies in the Hebrew Bible." *Journal of Biblical Literature* 125, no. 2 (2006): 225–41. doi:10.2307/27638359.

Levenson, Jon D., and Baruch Halpern. "The Political Import of David's Marriages." *Journal of Biblical Literature* 99, no. 4 (December 1980): 507–17. doi:10.2307/3265190.

Levine, Baruch A. "Religion in the Heroic Spirit: Themes in the Book of Judges." In *Thus Says the Lord: Essays on the Former and Latter Prophets in honor of Robert R. Wilson*, edited by John J. Ahn and Stephen L. Cook, 27–42. New York: T&T Clark, 2009.

Liverani, Mario. *Myth and Politics in Ancient Near Eastern Historiography*. Edited by Zainab Bahrani and Marc Van De Mieroop. New York: Cornell University Press, 2004.

Măcelaru, Marcel V. "Saul in the Company of Men: (De)constructing Masculinity in 1 Samuel 9–31." In *Biblical Masculinities Foregrounded*, edited by Ovidiu Creangă and Peter-Ben Smit, 51–68. Hebrew Bible Monographs 62. Sheffield: Sheffield Phoenix Press, 2017.

Murphy, Kelly J. "Masculinity, Moral Agency, and Memory: The Spirit of the Deity in Judges, Samuel, and Beyond." *Journal of the Bible and its Reception* 2 (2015): 175–96. doi:10.1515/jbr-2015-0007.

Niditch, Susan. *Judges: A Commentary*. The Old Testament Library. Louisville: Westminster John Knox Press, 2008.

Peleg, Yaron. "Love at First Sight? David, Jonathan, and the Biblical Politics of Gender." *Journal for the Study of the Old Testament* 30, no. 2 (2005): 171–89. doi:10.1177/0309089205060606.

Polak, Frank H. "King, Spear and Arrow in the Saul-David Narratives." In *Seitenblicke: Literarische und historische Studien zu Nebenfiguren im zweiten Samuelbuch*, edited by Walter Dietrich, 53–70. Orbis Biblicus et Orientalis 249. Freiburg: Academic Press; Göttingen: Vandenhoeck & Ruprecht, 2011.

Prouser, Ora Horn. "Suited to the Throne: The Symbolic Use of Clothing in the David and Saul Narratives." *Journal for the Study of the Old Testament* 71 (1996): 27–37. doi:10.1177/030908929602107103.

Schrock, Douglas, and Michael Schwalbe. "Men, Masculinity, and Manhood Acts." *Annual Review of Sociology* 35 (2009): 277–95. doi:10.1146/annurev-soc-070308-115933.

Schroer, Silvia, and Thomas Staubli. "Saul, David, und Jonatan—eine Dreiecksgeschichte?: Ein Beitrag zum Thema 'Homosexualität im Ersten Testament'." *Bibel und Kirche* 51 (1996): 15–22.

Seebass, Horst. "Bosh." In *Theological Dictionary of the Old Testament*, edited by G. Johannes Botterweck and Helmer Ringgren and translated by John T. Willis, vol. 2, 50–60. Grand Rapids, MI: Eerdmans, 1977.

Stiebert, Johanna. *First-Degree Incest and the Hebrew Bible: Sex in the Family*. Library of Hebrew Bible/Old Testament Studies 596. London and New York: T&T Clark, 2016.

Stone, Ken. "Marriage and Sexual Relations in the World of the Hebrew Bible." In *The Oxford Handbook of Theology, Sexuality, and Gender*, edited by Adrian Thatcher, 175–87. Oxford: Oxford University Press, 2015. doi:10.1093/oxfordhb/9780199664153.013.020.

Thiede, Barbara. *Male Friendship, Homosociality, and Women of the Hebrew Bible: Malignant Fraternities*. Routledge Studies in the Biblical World 5. London and New York: Routledge, 2022. doi:10.4324/9780429326226.

Wilson, Stephen M. *Making Men: The Male Coming-of-Age Theme in the Hebrew Bible*. New York: Oxford University Press, 2015.

Hidden in Plain Sight—The Rape Culture of the Hebrew Bible
Conclusions

What is implicit avoids critique. By its very nature, it goes underexamined. "[T]he power of ideology," as Roland Boer writes, "increases in a direct ratio to its ability to remain hidden, to seem natural and part of the way things are" (2011, 43).

Ideology explains why biblical writers have no specific word for rape. Ideology explains why they offer no concept of consent. Hebrew Bible narratives make sexual violence of all kinds "part of the way things are." Biblical authors understand sexual violence as a powerful means for negotiating hierarchy and power, a means to an end. Female characters, male characters, and characters whose gender identity and performance fall outside of neat binaries are all victims of sexual violence in the Hebrew Bible; they can be and are raped in its pages.

The Hebrew Bible depicts an honor society, one in which the performance of masculinity depends on continued demonstrations of power, strength, and virility. Male characters must prove, again and again, that they are "good at being men."[1] Biblical authors proselytize on behalf of a hegemonic masculinity in which dominant males acquire honor, status, glory, and authority over other men. Such men are successful warriors both on the battlefield and in the bedroom. They acquire women's bodies and they father sons. They sexually humiliate and shame their enemies. Providing proof of masculinity features constant and often violent competitions for rank and clout. This is a volatile enterprise; those in positions of power may find themselves dead at the hands of those they believed vanquished. Still, biblical authors describe when male characters fail at the performance of ideal masculinity in order to make clear what is needed to succeed at it.

Yhwh, the Israelite deity, is the ultimate male role model and ruler. Yhwh, too, repeatedly proves his manhood in a range of settings, and he does so violently. He has no qualms about exercising his capacity for sexualized violence against any character or people he punishes. Foreign rulers are

DOI: 10.4324/9781003014911-5

made impotent and publicly humiliated (Gen. 12 and 20). Foreign deities are mutilated and cast aside (1 Sam. 5:3–4). Female characters are handed from one man to another at Yhwh's will (2 Sam. 12:8).

Yhwh's people, *am Yisrael* (עם ישראל), consists of the men who serve him. But his men can be feminized, personified as his female lover or bride. When they are, Yhwh is permitted, even justified, in invoking brutal punishment for any apparent act of disloyalty. The Israelite deity is depicted as acting with righteous anger when he strips and exposes Israel and subjects her to a violent mob that may stone or stab her (Ezek. 16:27–41). Daughter Zion, a female personification of his people, is raped by the nations at Yhwh's will (Lam. 1:9–10). His former lovers Oholah (Samaria) and Oholibah (Jerusalem) are to be mutilated and stoned (Ezek. 23). Yhwh exercises no reservations in the use of sexual violence; it is an instrument for establishing his dominance, his power, and his rule.

Mortal rulers of Israel should be in Yhwh's image and in his likeness. They should act as he does. David is good at being a man because, like his deity, he knows no limits when waging war. Almost the first words in the Hebrew Bible about David define him as a "mighty man of valor" and a warrior (1 Sam. 16:18).[2] Indeed, Israel's finest king kills with aplomb, and those he slaughters include not merely men, but women and children as well (1 Sam. 27:9). He runs up an impressive body count (Clines 2009, 217) and, in the course of his many battles, manages to enslave whole peoples (2 Sam. 8:2–6, 13–14). David is Yhwh's most beloved king precisely because of his capacity for violence. As we have seen, he is an effective warrior who knows how to take and rape women and how to humiliate, degrade, and sexually shame his male enemies. He is a man after Yhwh's own heart.

Other men of the texts, who aspire to honor their rulers, must emulate, support, collude, and enable them. The taking and raping of female characters and the intentional sexual humiliation of male ones do not constitute merely a backdrop to political events. Such deeds *are* political. They constitute the core of the narratives. They must do so in a literary world in which sexual violence is the instrument for establishing power, authority, and rule.

In the Books of Samuel, dominant men establish their status and rank by taking and raping women. Other men aspire to do the same or, at least, demonstrate loyalty to king and deity by colluding, collaborating, and sanctioning the sexual violence their rulers commit. Family and kinship conflicts are worked out through the use of violence. Male-male alliances and friendships function similarly. Rapists are supported by a company of men, even an army of them. Servants, messengers, courtiers, soldiers, generals, advisors—all help move, direct, control, and sexually exploit women. They are essential to biblical rape culture.

Dominant men cement their ties through sexual violence against other men too. Their most effective proof of superiority lies in shaming enemies sexually. Men penetrate one another with weapons that serve as symbols for their own members; they cut off their enemies' heads, hands, and even foreskins. Here, too, the man who sexually humiliates his enemy is supported by other men. In fact, as we have seen, the king who has not proven that he deserves his men's support through powerful displays of sexual violence is a failed king.

Sexual violence proves authority, virility, and potency. Men can and even should take and rape women in full view of other men (2 Sam. 16:22). They sexually humiliate other men in public too (10:4). Sexual violence does not take place behind closed doors; it is a shared experience. In 2 Samuel 11, 13, and 16, biblical authors offer scenes of men sharing women's bodies in speech, thought, and deed. Female characters are ogled by men standing side by side. Men plan the rape of women with other men. They even arrange a rape so that other men may hear or watch them in the act. They prove their loyalty and bond through sharing the experience of sexual violence against women. The voyeurism male characters engage in supports biblical hegemonic masculinity; it is a necessary element in its expression.

Biblical authors make us look too. Readers must watch as Tamar is forced to become a sexual show for Amnon and his accomplices—both as she prepares his "love cakes" and afterwards, too, when she is brutally raped and thrown out of Amnon's rooms (2 Sam. 13). When Ahithophel advises Absalom to rape his father's women, we, too, imagine the rape about to happen, one that will be witnessed by all Israel (16:22).

We cannot ignore the sexual violence male characters experience either, violence that is presented graphically to the biblical audience—and to the modern reader. We can envision the Philistines dead on the battlefield and David and his men stripping and symbolically castrating their corpses, foreskins counted out and displayed before King Saul and his court (1 Sam. 18:27). We will watch as Joab and his men repeatedly pierce and penetrate Absalom as he hangs by the hair that once signified his potency (2 Sam. 18:14–15).

"Each society has its regime of truth," Michel Foucault has said, "its 'general politics' of truth: that is, the types of discourse which it accepts and makes function as true" (1977, 131). What is true in the discourse of the Books of Samuel is disturbing. We are witnesses to a literary rape culture that sanctions sexualized violence of all kinds.

The Hebrew Bible is hardly alone in presenting the modern reader with a rape culture. Biblical literature of all kinds features texts of terror and violence against a host of victims. The ills of hegemonic masculinity can be found also among the pages of New Testament texts, as well as of apocryphal ones, and scholars continue to work on calling out these ills for good reason.

But those scholars who insist that there can be no such thing as rape culture in the Hebrew Bible because its authors had no word for rape and no concept of consent must consider the repercussions of their claims. They are running the risk of aligning with authors who valorize sexual violence. They are helping to keep hidden what is very much there. They are assisting in making sexual violence the natural outcome of "the way things were." In what they imagine an important, even noble, effort to judge the text in its presumed historical context, they reinscribe the world view and toxic ideology of the authors. Such decisions have material consequences.

We are confronted with a rape culture in texts considered sacred and holy across the globe. Readers who themselves belong to rape cultures that valorize violence against women may pass over or ignore the import of the sexual violence portrayed in the Hebrew Bible and, as a result, collude in reinforcing and normalizing rape culture values. Certainly, it is in the interest of those who wield power in the rape cultures of our time that they do so. Bypassing sexual violence amounts to sanctioning it. The predators of our own time prosper in hegemonic systems that maximize their ability to sexually humiliate and degrade others—to rape them, in fact.

"Rape culture" is a term of resistance; it calls out what has been hidden, what has been normalized, what must be exposed and made explicit if we are to have any hope of living in a world in which sexual violence is not "part of the way things are." Modern readers can refuse to become bystanders and witnesses by noticing where we find rape cultures in the literature we read and by naming and revealing the inestimable damage such literary rape cultures can do.

This is not an easy task. For Jews, a critique of biblical hegemonic masculinity can call up visceral and historical trauma. For centuries, Christians have weaponized the Hebrew Bible against Jews, claiming that the "Old Testament" depicts an angry and violent god who was naturally superseded by the "loving god" of the New Testament. Only a stubborn and recalcitrant people could fail to accept that truth. Christians later added to their charges, accusing Jews of committing deicide, a myth that even today resists the complete eradication it deserves. Weaponizing the Hebrew Bible against Jews continues to threaten Jewish lives. It is essential to acknowledge not only the violence that is embedded in these texts but also the violence coming from those who exploit them to destructive, even murderous ends.

Clearly, no one can afford to downplay, bypass, or ignore the sexual violence of biblical texts. The consequences of doing so have been to reinscribe rape cultures across the globe for centuries. We must all come to grips with the painful hegemonic masculinities biblical literature often works to valorize. We must become attuned and become traitors to depictions and enactments of dominant, exploitative masculinity wherever we find it—for our own sakes, and regardless of our gender expression.[3] Scholars, religious leaders, teachers, and readers must choose not to be complicit. We must do the difficult and painful work of analyzing the dangerous ideologies underpinning biblical hegemonic masculinity. If we do not call out these texts for the violence they authorize and sanction, we give our tacit consent to the premises of the rape culture they depict and, by extension, to the rape cultures we ourselves inhabit. Those who suffer sexual violence in our own time will be the victims of our apathy, indifference, or denial. Instead, we must name the rape cultures we find in texts we call sacred, holy, or simply foundational. Doing so is a necessary step toward dismantling *every* rape culture, past and present. Hence, the writing of *Rape in the House of David: A Company of Men*, a work that seeks to contribute this very goal.

Notes

1 Anthropologist Michael Herzfeld coined this phrase in the singular. It became a staple in scholarly circles for good reason (1985, 16).
2 Clines 2009, 216. Clines models his ideal biblical man on David, a killer par excellence according to his reading.
3 In speaking with me about the need to invent masculinities that could be nourishing, tender, and gentle, Reuven McCullough suggested we must be "traitors" to those masculinities expressed through dominance and hierarchy. I paraphrased his formulation here in this text.

Bibliography

Boer, Roland. "The Patriarch's Nuts: Concerning the Testicular Logic of Biblical Hebrew." *Journal of Men, Masculinities, and Spirituality* 5, no. 2 (2011): 41–42.
Clines, David J.A. *Interested Parties: The Ideology of Writers and Readers of the Hebrew Bible*. Sheffield: Sheffield Phoenix Press, 2009.
Foucault, Michel. *Power and Knowledge: Selected Interviews & Other Writings 1972–1977*. Edited by Colin Gordon, translated by Colin Gordon, Leo Marshall, John Mepham, and Kate Soper. New York: Vintage Books, 1977.
Herzfeld, Michael. *The Politics of Manhood: Contest and Identity in a Cretan Mountain Village*. Princeton: Princeton University Press, 1985.

Author and Subject Index

Abasili, Alexander Izuchukwu 4–5, 6–7, 69n44
Abigail 43n48, 51, 91, 94
Abimelech (Genesis) 41n35, 67n23
Abner 51–3, 59, 62–3, 91
Abraham 94n17
Absalom 3, 14, 23–5, 27, 28, 32, 33, 34, 35–8, 39n8, 41n25, 41n27, 41n28, 41n30, 41n35, 42n37, 42n38, 42n40, 42n42, 43n50, 53, 58, 63–4, 93n23, 96n44, 102
Ackerman, Susan 95n36, 96n42
Adonijah 24, 67n19, 93n8, 94n23
adultery 60, 64, 69n40, 70n59
Ahasuerus 59
Ahimelech 90
Ahinoam (Saul's Wife) 67n15, 88, 89, 91, 92
Ahinoam of Jezreel (David's Wife) 39n8, 51, 90, 91, 92, 96n52
Ahithophel 35–7, 42n45, 42n47, 102
Alter, Robert 31, 33, 40n12, 41n35, 66n4, 68n34, 75, 76, 88
Amalek 66n7
Amalekites 78, 91
Amasa 63
Amnon 3, 5, 14, 23–35, 38, 39n8, 40n9, 40n10, 40n12, 40n13, 41n25, 41n27, 41n32, 41n34, 53, 55, 60, 61, 69n41, 70n58, 77, 83, 102
Andruska, Jennifer 59, 69n42
ark 53–4, 56, 62
Ashkenasy, Nehama 66n4, 66n10
Astour, Michael C. 43n48
Avioz, Michael 94n23

Bakon, Shimon 25
Bal, Mieke 17n10
Barak 79
Bathsheba 3, 5, 6, 14, 23, 25, 26, 36, 40n14, 42n43, 42n45, 46, 55, 56–65, 68n33, 68n34, 68n37, 69n44, 69n48, 70n54, 70n58, 70n60, 94n23
Baumgartner, Walter 50, 67n14, 67n15
Benjamin, Don C. 25, 39n5, 41n27
Benjamin(ites) 6, 18n21, 18n23, 53, 66n8, 75, 76
Berkovits, Eliezer 18n22
Bernstein, J.M. 12
Bilhah 42n46
Bird, Sharon R. 39n6
biryah 26, 27
Bledstein, Adrien Janis 17n10
Blyth, Caroline 69n45
Boer, Roland 66n12, 94n20, 100
Boswell, A. Ayers 39n6
Bows, Hannah 17n5

Chapman, Cynthia R. 68n30, 74, 79, 83, 93n1, 95n30, 96n43
Clines, David J.A. 22, 42n36, 67n24, 67n25, 83, 93n4, 93n6, 94n22, 101, 104n2
Comforth, Tracee 69n48
Connell, R.W. 22

Da Silva, Teresa 14, 18n33
Deborah 79
Dietrich, Walter 40n23
Dinah 4, 69n41, 69n46
Dunn, Suzie 16n1, 16n2, 68n38, 89

Author and Subject Index

Ehud 2
Eliab 66n11, 82, 94n23, 94n24, 95n28
Eliam 36, 57
Engelken, Karen 33, 34
ephod 54
Esther 59
Exum, J. Cheryl 13, 49, 57, 59, 64, 65, 66n4, 68n26, 68n32, 69n47, 69n48, 94n10

feminization 12, 49, 56, 63, 74, 77, 79, 82, 83, 84, 89, 93, 101
Fewell, Danna Nolan 41n23
Firth, David G. 67n15
Flood, Michael 30, 39n6, 41n34, 70n52, 70n55
Fokkelman, J.P. 42n37, 67n22, 68n31, 68n36
foreskin(s) 2, 12, 49, 53, 74, 85, 92, 102
Foucault, Michel 102
Frymer-Kensky, Tikva 40n14, 42n45, 68n37, 69n48, 70n59
Fuchs, Esther 39n2, 66n4, 66n10

Gailey, Jeannine A. 39n6, 40n19
gender 1, 16, 18n30, 30, 31, 34, 39n4, 89, 96n49, 100, 104
Gibeah 76
Gilmore, David D. 74
Goliath 42n38, 47, 50, 51, 53, 67n16, 81–6, 90, 92, 94n21, 95n29, 95n32
Graybill, Rhiannon 17n10, 17n15, 17n19, 95n35
Greenough, Chris 93n3
Grossman, Jonathan 37
Guest, Deryn 17n9, 17n10, 70n58
Gunn, David M. 41n23

Haddox, Susan 17n10
Halperin, David M. 32, 94n11
Halpern, Baruch 42n45, 67n15, 96n52
Hammond, Dorothy 94n11
Harding, James E. 18n29, 95n36, 96n42, 96n48
Harkins, Leigh 14, 18n33
Hawkins, Ralph 93n9
hegemonic masculinity 1, 28, 29, 31, 32, 46, 62, 63, 64, 100, 102, 103, 104

Hertzberg, H.W. 68n34
Herzfeld, Michael 104n1
Higgins, Ryan S. 40n18
Hill, Andrew E. 33
Hiram 53
homoeroticism 32, 54, 84, 85, 87
homosexuality 17n13, 96n48
homosociality 14, 22, 39n6, 41n34, 62, 66n2, 70n55, 70n56, 89
honor 12, 13, 22, 23, 27, 28, 29, 32, 34, 35, 36, 37, 30n5, 41n27, 46, 48, 50, 51, 52, 53, 54, 55, 56, 57, 63, 64, 65, 66n2, 67n24, 70n54, 70n61, 74, 77, 80, 83, 95n38, 100, 101
Hummer, Robert A. 39n6
Hushai 36–7

incest 40n9, 41n25, 96n46
Isaac 17n17, 41n35, 67n23, 94n17
Ish-bosheth 52–3, 59, 91

Jablow, Alta 94n11
Jennings, Theodore W. 54, 67n21, 94n11, 96n42
Jesse 66n11, 81, 82, 87, 91, 95n41
Joab 23, 25, 38, 43n50, 52, 53, 55, 57, 59, 60, 61, 62–3, 65, 74, 93n8, 102
Jonadab 24–6, 27, 28–9, 30, 31, 35, 40n13, 41n29, 55
Jonathan 13, 33, 40n22, 42n39, 47, 50, 51, 56, 66n5, 78, 79, 84, 85–9, 91, 92, 95n36, 95n39, 95n40, 96n46, 96n48
Joseph 40n15, 67n23

Kalmanofsky, Amy 40n13, 40n17, 41n25
Kaluzny, Gretchen 68n35
Kawashima, Robert S. 4, 7, 9, 10
Kessler, Gwynn 9
Koehler, Ludwig 50, 67n14, 67n15
Koenig, Sara M. 56, 69n42, 69n48

Laban 43n48
Langlamet, F. 34
Lawrence, Beatrice 17n15
Lazarewicz-Wyrzykowska, Ela 93n2, 94n13
lechem 26, 40n15

Lemos, T.M. 93n2, 95n33
Leneman, Helen 69n48
Léturneau, Anne 59, 69n42, 69n48
Levenson, Jon Douglas 42n45, 67n15, 96n52
Levine, Baruch 50, 94n14
Lipka, Hilary 5, 6
Liverani, Mario 77, 94n16

Măcelaru, Marcel V. 93n5, 95n38
Matthews, Victor H. 25, 39n5, 41n27
Merab 48, 49, 66n3
Michal 14, 28, 46–55, 59, 60, 62, 63, 65, 66n3, 66n4, 67n22, 68n26, 84, 85, 86, 90, 91, 92, 95n37
Minister, Meredith 17n15
Mizpah 76
Moabites 56
Moses 18n30
Murnen, Sarah K. 68n35
Murphy, Kelly J. 77, 78

Nabal 51, 67n15, 91, 96n53
Nagouse, Emma 2
Nathan 42n44, 88
necromancer 79
Nicol, George G. 68n34
Niditch, Susan 2, 17n11, 17n21, 74

Olyan, Saul M. 25, 40n12, 41n29, 41n30

Paltiel 47, 53, 60, 62, 65, 68n26, 91
Pease, Bob 41n34
Peleg, Yaron 66n4, 95n36, 96n48
Peters, Kurtis 40n23
Philistines 48, 49, 50, 53, 56, 78–80, 82, 83, 84, 85, 90, 92, 102
pilegesh/pilagshim 3, 14, 17n12, 18n32, 23–4, 31, 33–8, 41, 42n46, 43n49, 52, 53, 55, 56, 58, 59, 64, 66n6, 68n28, 68n29, 79, 80, 94n19, 95n41
Polak, Frank H. 94n20
Potiphar 40n15, 67n23
Probyn, Elspeth 41n31

Author and Subject Index 107

Prohaska, Ariane 39n6, 40n19
prophet(s) 42n44, 55, 76, 78, 79, 80, 86–7
Propp, William H. 39n5
Prouser, Ora Horn 95n38

Rabinowitz, Jacob J. 69n40
rape culture(s) 1, 2, 3, 6–8, 10, 11, 14, 15, 16, 17n13, 22, 23, 28, 31, 35, 37, 39, 42n42, 46, 55, 57, 59, 60, 61, 62, 64, 65, 66, 75, 88, 89, 93, 96n48, 100–4
Rebekah 17n17, 18n30
Rey, M.I. 18n24
Rizpah 52–3, 66n6, 91
Roth, Martha T. 69n40
ruach 77
ruach Elohim 77–8
ruach ra'ah 81
Rubin, Gayle S. 40n11
Rudman, Dominic 41n28
Ruth 11, 61, 67n24, 95n26

sacrifice, sacrificing 63, 66n7, 77, 78, 80, 87, 94n17
Samuel 47, 49, 66n11, 75, 76, 77, 78–9, 80, 86, 94n21, 94n24
Sanders, Seth 31, 42n38
Scholz, Susanne 2, 6, 17n8, 67n23, 68n34
Schorch, Stefan 70n51
Schrock, Douglas 94n15
Schroeder, Joy A. 11
Schroer, Silvia 96n42, 96n48
Schulte, Leah Rediger 4, 5, 6
Schwalbe, Michael 94n15
Schwartz, Regina M. 70n59
Sedgwick, Eve Kosofsky 39n4
Seebass, Horst 88, 96n48
Shechem 11, 69n41, 69n46
Shepherd, David 11
Shiloh 18n21, 66n8
Shimei 36
Sisera 2, 79
Sisera's mother 67n17
Solomon 3, 24, 58, 67n19, 93n8

Southwood, Katherine E. 18n21
Staubli, Thomas 96n42, 96n48
Stiebert, Johanna 96n46
Spade, Joan Z. 39n6
Steussy, Marti J. 68n33
Stone, Ken 26, 30, 34–5, 39n5, 40n9, 41n24, 41n32, 41n33, 42n42, 52, 57, 63, 64, 66n2, 66n10, 68n27, 70n53, 70n54, 70n60, 95n34

Tamar 3, 5, 6, 14, 22, 23, 24–31, 32, 33, 34, 35, 38, 40n13, 41n25, 41n27, 41n28, 41n34, 41n35, 53, 55, 56, 61, 63, 68n29, 69n41, 77, 83, 94n23, 102
Thiede, Barbara 17n6, 17n14, 18n31, 18n32, 26, 39n7, 41n30, 41n35, 43n49, 67n15, 67n23, 68n28, 69n43, 70n61, 81, 87, 95n25, 95n29, 95n36, 95n41
Tombs, David 42n40
Trible, Phyllis 39n8, 41n28

Uriah 23, 26, 42n43, 56, 57, 60–3, 64, 65, 66n9, 69n44, 70n54, 70n56, 70n57

Van Dijk-Hemmes, Fokkelien 40n9, 40n13, 40n17
Van Selms, A. 25
van Wolde, Ellen 17n10, 66n4
Vermeule, Emily 17n11

Washington, Harold C. 3, 17n20, 18n22, 18n28, 41n35
Weishut, Daniel J.N. 18n27
West, Gerald O. 18n26
Westbrook, Raymond 69n40
Wilson, Stephen M. 39n1, 83–4, 94n11, 95n32
Woodhams, Jessica 14, 18n33
Wright, Carrie 68n35
Wright, G.R.H. 43n48

Yancey Martin, Patricia 39n6
Yee, Gale A. 32, 17n10, 70n56

Index of Biblical References

Dan. 9:9 88

Deut. 15 9
Deut. 20:10–20 67
Deut. 21 9
Deut. 21:10–14 6, 8, 9, 11
Deut. 22 7
Deut. 22:8 68
Deut. 22:13 41
Deut. 22:22 4, 69
Deut. 22:22–24 60
Deut. 22:23–25 4
Deut. 22:25 52
Deut. 22:28–29 4, 41
Deut. 24:1 95
Deut. 24:3 41

Esther 1:19 59
Esther 2:2 58
Esther 2:2–4 59
Esther 5:2 95
Esther 7:3 95

Exod. 4:25 61
Exod. 22:15 69

Ezek. 2:3 88
Ezek. 16:15–43 93
Ezek. 16:27–41 2, 66, 89, 101
Ezek. 16:57 77
Ezek. 23 2, 101
Ezek. 23:1–49 93
Ezek. 23:17–21 89
Ezek. 23:22–44 6
Ezek. 33:31–32 42

Gen. 3:7 95
Gen. 12 2, 66, 70, 101
Gen. 18:25 42
Gen. 19 2
Gen. 19:8 2, 50, 66
Gen. 20 70, 101
Gen. 20:9 69
Gen. 22 94
Gen. 24 18
Gen. 24:58–59 17
Gen. 26 2, 70
Gen. 26:8 41, 67
Gen. 27:9 41
Gen. 31 43
Gen. 34 69
Gen. 34:1 11
Gen. 34:2 11, 69
Gen. 38 43
Gen. 38:2 55
Gen. 39:6 40
Gen. 39:14 67
Gen. 41:2, 5, 7, 19, 20 40
Gen. 49:4 42

Hosea 2:5 9, 89
Hosea 2:12–13 17, 93

Isa. 6:2 61
Isa. 7:20 61, 68
Isa. 10:32 13
Isa. 13:8 48
Isa. 26:17 48
Isa. 43:7 67
Isa. 47:3 9, 77, 89
Isa. 57:8 13

Index of Biblical References

Jer. 4:31 48
Jer. 13:20–27 89
Jer. 38:19 94
Jer. 51:30 74, 83

Job 30:11 2

Josh. 2:8 68
Josh. 22:16, 18–19 88

Judg. 1:6–7 2
Judg. 3:21–22 2
Judg. 4 2
Judg. 4:8–9, 21 79
Judg. 5 2
Judg. 5:26–27 79
Judg. 5:30 67
Judg. 9:53 79
Judg. 10 49
Judg. 11 77
Judg. 11:34–39 77
Judg. 19 2, 77
Judg. 19:2 95
Judg. 19:24 2, 50, 66
Judg. 19:25 2, 52, 79
Judg. 19:29 2
Judg. 19:29–30 94
Judg. 20 77
Judg. 21 6, 7
Judg. 21:11–12 67
Judg. 21 17
Judg. 21:20 66
Judg. 21:20–23 2, 18, 66

Lam. 1:9–10 66, 89, 101
Lam. 3 2

Lev. 15:18 69
Lev. 18:6–18 95
Lev. 18:22 69
Lev. 19:20–22 17
Lev. 20:13 69

Mic. 1:11 96
Mic. 4:10 48

Nah. 3:5 9
Nah. 3:5–6 89

Num. 31:17–18 67

Prov. 30:20 40

Ruth 2:2, 10, 13 95
Ruth 3:8 61
Ruth 4:11 67

1 Kings 1:4 42
1 Kings 2:22–25 67
1 Kings 2:25 93
1 Kings 2:34 62, 93
1 Kings 9:21 93
1 Kings 11:3 3, 58, 93
1 Kings 12:10 61

2 Kings 10:6–11 95

1 Sam. 8:7 76
1 Sam. 8:20 47, 80, 81
1 Sam. 9:1 75
1 Sam. 9:2 66, 67, 75
1 Sam. 9:6 76
1 Sam. 9:21 80
1 Sam. 10 87
1 Sam. 10:10 81, 94
1 Sam. 10:11 87
1 Sam. 10:17–22, 24, 26–27 76
1 Sam. 11 56, 95
1 Sam. 11:1–2 77
1 Sam. 11:2 56
1 Sam. 11:6 77, 94
1 Sam. 11:6–7, 11 77
1 Sam. 11:12–13 80
1 Sam. 13:3, 8, 9, 13–14 78, 79
1 Sam. 13:8–9 78, 80
1 Sam. 13:9–14 66
1 Sam. 13:13–14 80
1 Sam. 13:22 85
1 Sam. 14 66, 94
1 Sam. 14:1–15 85
1 Sam. 14:24 66, 78
1 Sam. 14:46 78
1 Sam. 14:47–48 95
1 Sam. 14:49 66, 91, 94
1 Sam. 14:50 51, 91
1 Sam. 15:8–9 66
1 Sam. 15:11 80
1 Sam. 15:20–21 78

1 Sam. 16 67, 94
1 Sam. 16:6 94
1 Sam. 16:6–7, 8–12 66
1 Sam. 16:12 49, 50, 67, 81, 94
1 Sam. 16:13 49
1 Sam. 16:14 81
1 Sam. 16:18 81, 101
1 Sam. 16:21 84
1 Sam. 16:22 81
1 Sam. 17 67, 94
1 Sam. 17:13 95
1 Sam. 17:17–18, 20–24, 26, 33, 42 82
1 Sam. 17:26–27, 30 42
1 Sam. 17:33–35, 39–40 83
1 Sam. 17:45–47 53
1 Sam. 17:46 50
1 Sam. 17:50 2, 83, 86
1 Sam. 17:51 2, 84, 86
1 Sam. 18 47, 66, 91
1 Sam. 18:1 84
1 Sam. 18:2, 4–7 85
1 Sam. 18:5–7, 20 84
1 Sam. 18:6–9 48
1 Sam. 18:7 81
1 Sam. 18:10–11 48, 80
1 Sam. 18:19 48
1 Sam. 18:20 47, 48, 83
1 Sam. 18:20–21 48
1 Sam. 18:20–27 47
1 Sam. 18:21 47, 49
1 Sam. 18:22–23, 25–8 49
1 Sam. 18:27 2, 49, 53, 85, 86, 102
1 Sam. 19 66
1 Sam. 19:1 50, 86
1 Sam. 19:3–4 66
1 Sam. 19:4–7 50
1 Sam. 19:5 86
1 Sam. 19:8–10 50
1 Sam. 19:9–10 80
1 Sam. 19:11 50, 70
1 Sam. 19:11–16 95
1 Sam. 19:12 50
1 Sam. 19:17 50
1 Sam. 19:20, 21, 24 86
1 Sam. 20:6 87
1 Sam. 20:8 42
1 Sam. 20:13 42, 87
1 Sam. 20:17, 28, 30–31 87
1 Sam. 20:20 3

Index of Biblical References 111

1 Sam. 20:31 88
1 Sam. 20:33 80
1 Sam. 20:33–34, 41–42 90
1 Sam. 21:5–6 90
1 Sam. 22:1–2, 9–10 90
1 Sam. 22:17–19 78, 90
1 Sam. 23:1–13 90
1 Sam. 24:4–8 40
1 Sam. 25 43, 66, 90
1 Sam. 25:39–42 91
1 Sam. 25:44 47, 51, 91
1 Sam. 26:11–25 40
1 Sam. 26:12 80
1 Sam. 27:9 101
1 Sam. 28:3, 6–7, 9, 10–11, 13–14, 17–19 79
1 Sam. 30:2–3, 16–18 91
1 Sam. 31:4 79, 80, 84, 94
1 Sam. 31:8–9 74
1 Sam. 31:9 84
1 Sam. 31:9–10 81

2 Sam. 1 51
2 Sam. 1:14–15 40
2 Sam. 2 52
2 Sam. 2:8 52
2 Sam. 3 66
2 Sam. 3:1 51, 91
2 Sam. 3:2 51
2 Sam. 3:2–3 39
2 Sam. 3:2–5 91
2 Sam. 3:2–7, 11–14 52
2 Sam. 3:6–7 52
2 Sam. 3:14 91
2 Sam. 3:14–15 47
2 Sam. 3:16–18 53
2 Sam. 3:27 53, 62, 63
2 Sam. 3:28 40
2 Sam. 3:29 74
2 Sam. 4:2, 5–8, 9, 11 53
2 Sam. 4:5–8, 12 91
2 Sam. 4:7–8 2
2 Sam. 4:8 95
2 Sam. 4:11 40
2 Sam. 5:1–3 92
2 Sam. 5:9 53
2 Sam. 5:11 53
2 Sam. 5:13–25 53
2 Sam. 6 56, 66

Index of Biblical References

2 Sam. 6:15 67
2 Sam. 6:21–22 54
2 Sam. 6:23 47, 55
2 Sam. 7:16 34
2 Sam. 8:1–6, 13–14 95
2 Sam. 8:2, 3–6 56
2 Sam. 8:2–6, 13–14 95, 101
2 Sam. 9:1–10 56
2 Sam. 10:2–5 56
2 Sam. 10:4 35, 55, 102
2 Sam. 10:5 35, 83
2 Sam. 11 26, 27, 39, 55. 56, 70, 103
2 Sam. 11:1 57, 68
2 Sam. 11:1–3 57
2 Sam. 11:1–4 55
2 Sam. 11:2–4 3
2 Sam. 11:3 36
2 Sam. 11:4 59
2 Sam. 11:5–6 60
2 Sam. 11:7–8, 10–11 61
2 Sam. 11:11, 13, 15 62
2 Sam. 11:16–17 63
2 Sam. 11:25 63
2 Sam. 12:7–8 88
2 Sam. 12:8 59, 65, 66, 67
2 Sam. 12:9 57
2 Sam. 12:10–12 64
2 Sam. 12:11 88
2 Sam. 12:11–12 34, 42
2 Sam. 13 6, 39, 102
2 Sam. 13:1 24, 27
2 Sam. 13:2 24
2 Sam. 13:3 25, 38
2 Sam. 13:4 27
2 Sam. 13:5 25, 26
2 Sam. 13:6 25
2 Sam. 13:7 25, 29
2 Sam. 13:8 29
2 Sam. 13:9 29–30
2 Sam. 13:11 30
2 Sam. 13:13 38, 77
2 Sam. 13:14 30, 52, 83
2 Sam. 13:15–18 30
2 Sam. 13:19–20 28
2 Sam. 13:20 25, 28
2 Sam. 13:21 27
2 Sam. 13:23–25 28
2 Sam. 13:26–27 28
2 Sam. 13:30–31 28
2 Sam. 13:32 28, 31
2 Sam. 14:25 27
2 Sam. 14:33 32
2 Sam. 15:1, 4 31
2 Sam. 15:5 32
2 Sam. 15:12 36
2 Sam. 15:13 33
2 Sam. 15:16 33, 34
2 Sam. 15:17–18 33
2 Sam. 15:20 33
2 Sam. 15:21 42
2 Sam. 15:22 33
2 Sam. 15:31, 32 36
2 Sam. 15:32 36
2 Sam. 16 102
2 Sam. 16:8 36
2 Sam. 16:16–17, 20–21 37
2 Sam. 16:22 23, 37, 58, 96, 102
2 Sam. 16:23 36
2 Sam. 17:1, 11 37
2 Sam. 18:12–13 43
2 Sam. 18:14 38, 63
2 Sam. 18:14–15 102
2 Sam. 20:10 63
2 Sam. 20:21–22 95
2 Sam. 21:8–9 66
2 Sam. 23 36
2 Sam. 23:8–39 36
2 Sam. 23:10 74
2 Sam. 23:34 36, 58